Coloring Book for Adults

Butterflies

and

Blossoms

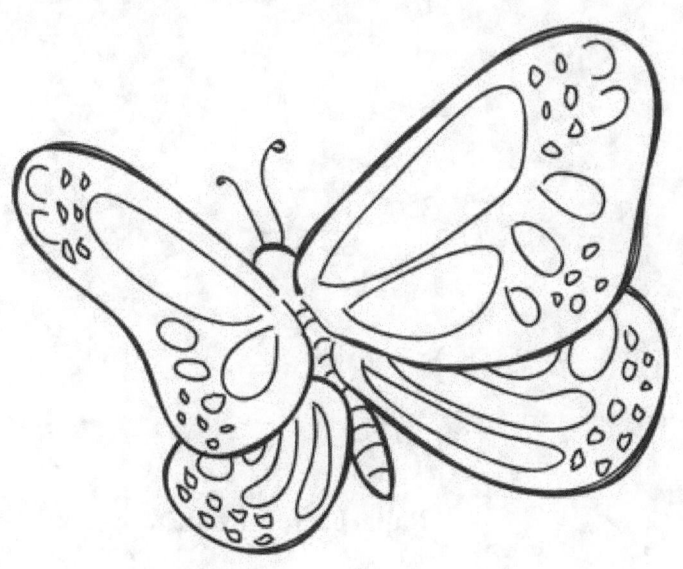

By: Julia Brockmann

ISBN-13: 978-1523261543

PUBLISHERS NOTES

Disclaimer

Published by

InfoEbooksOnline.com

Paperback Edition

Manufactured in the United States of America

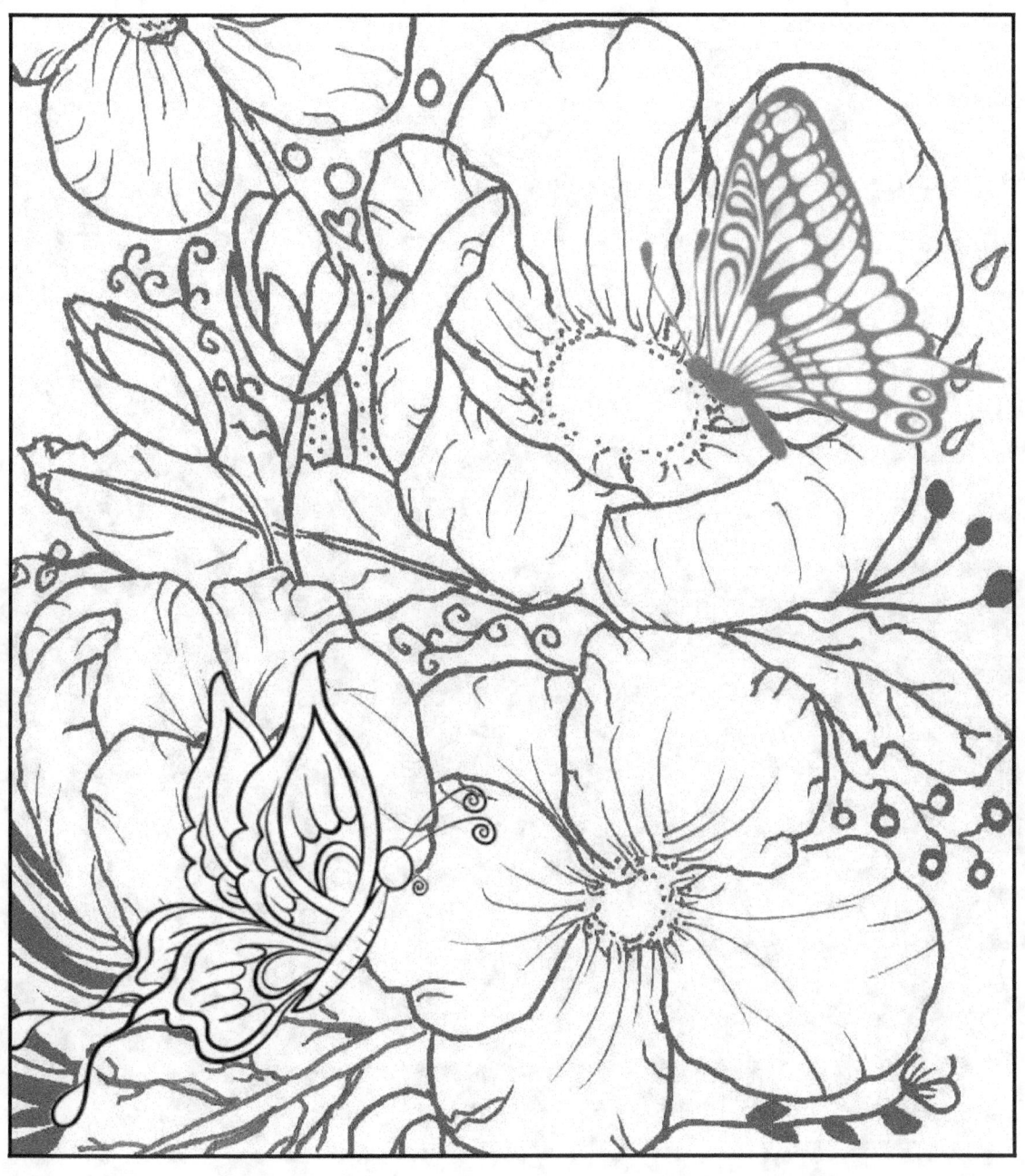

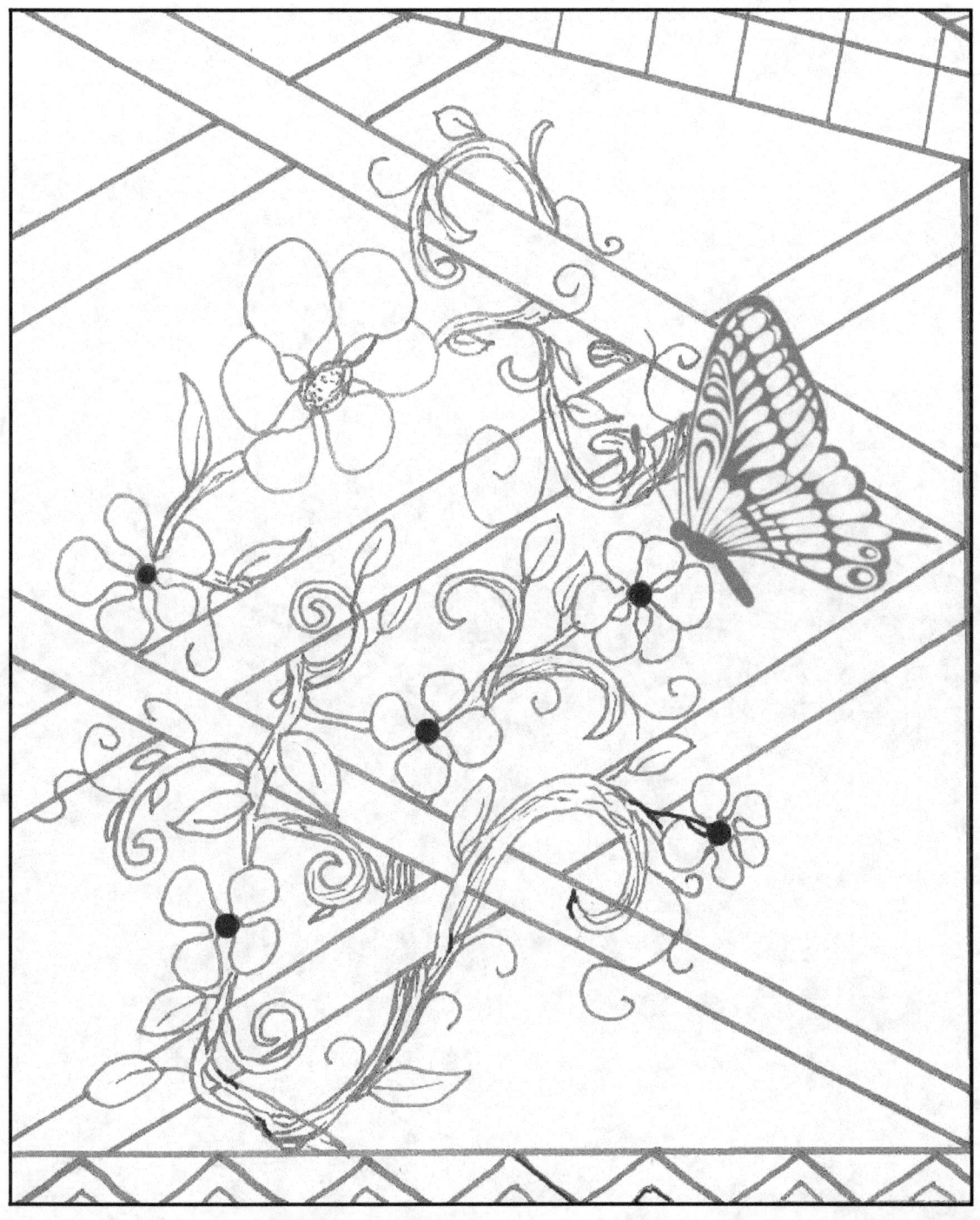

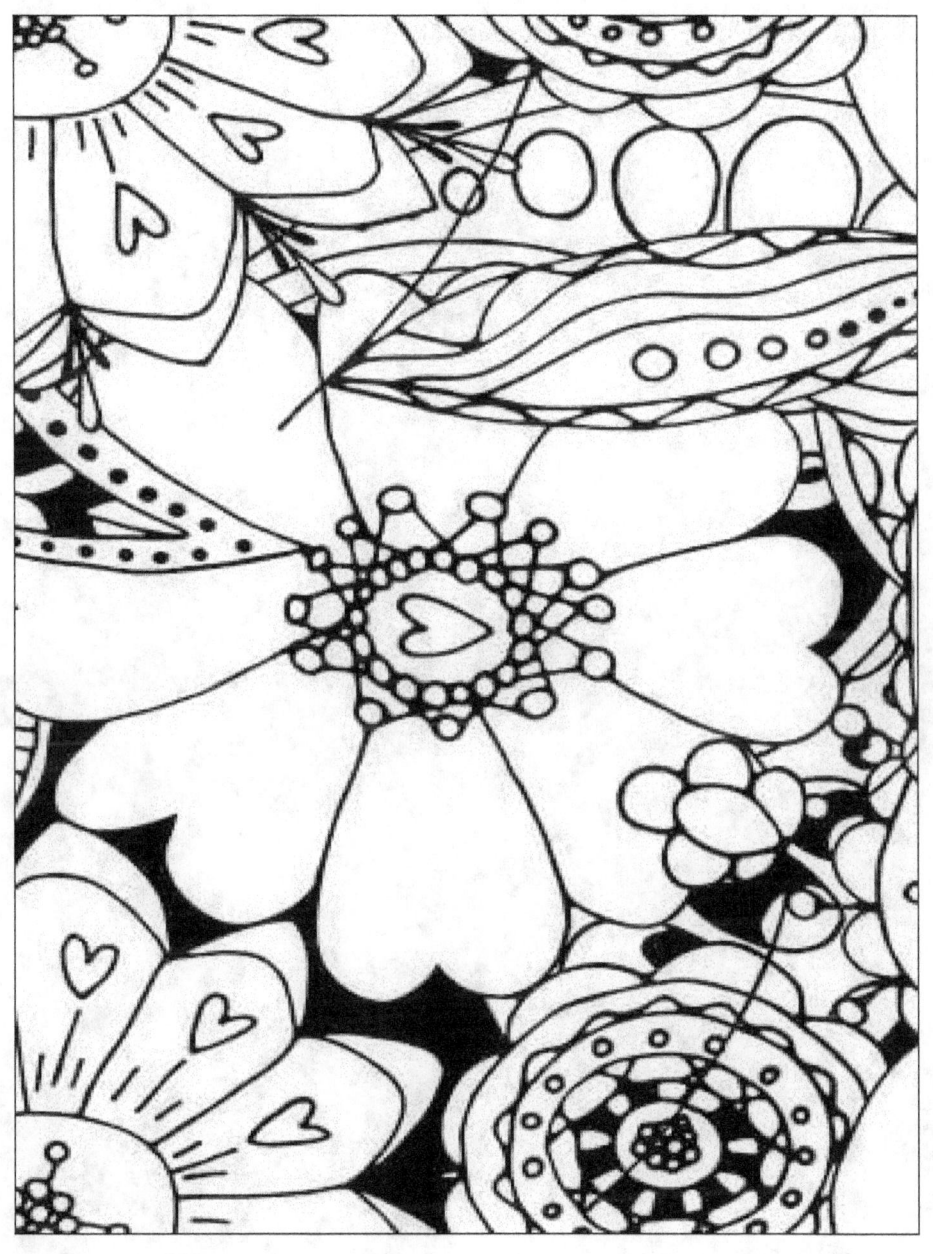

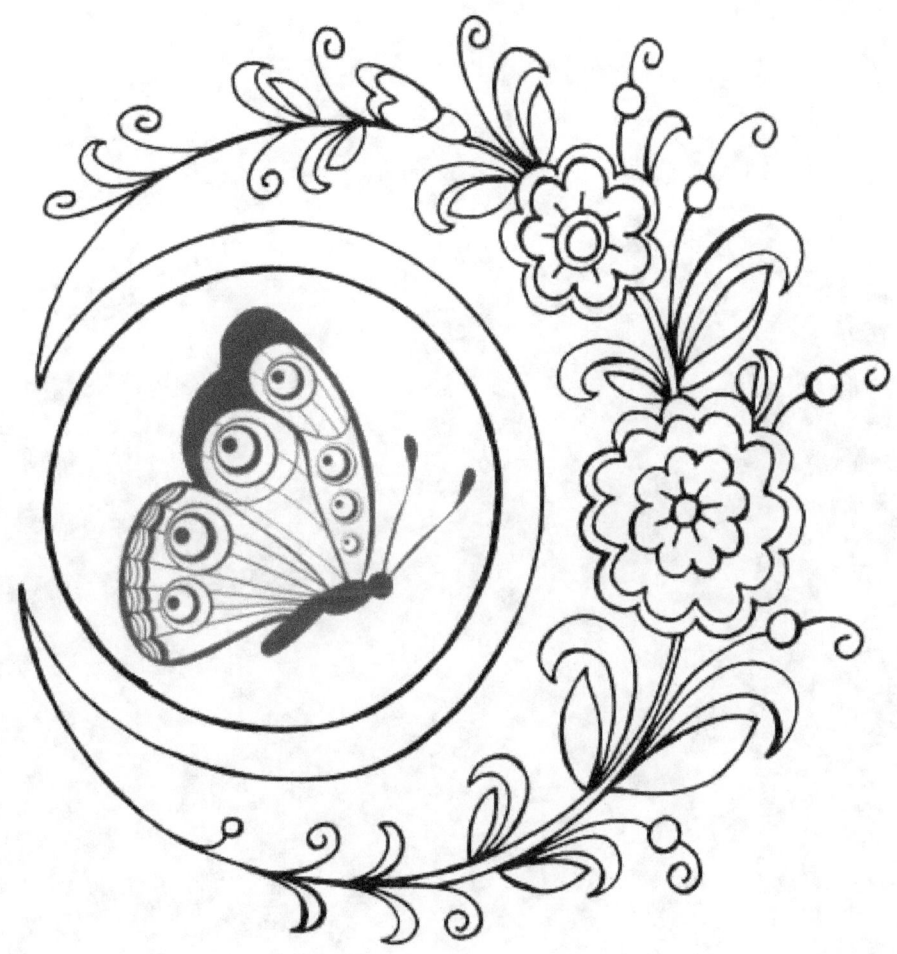

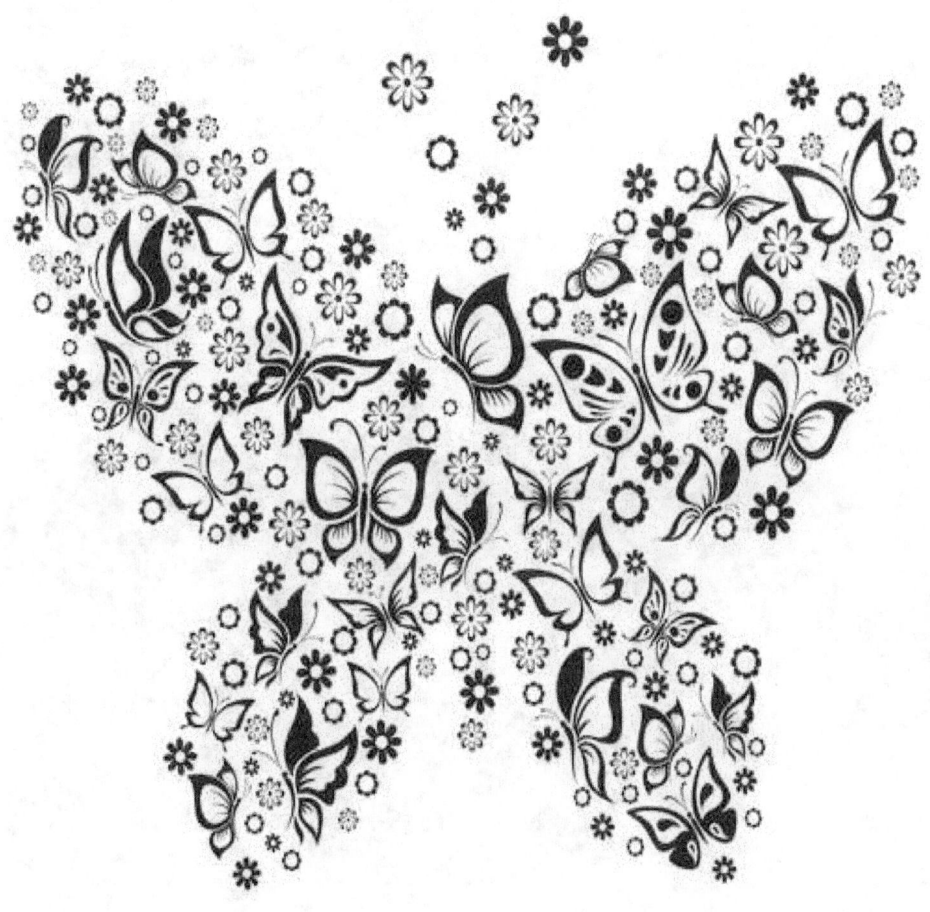

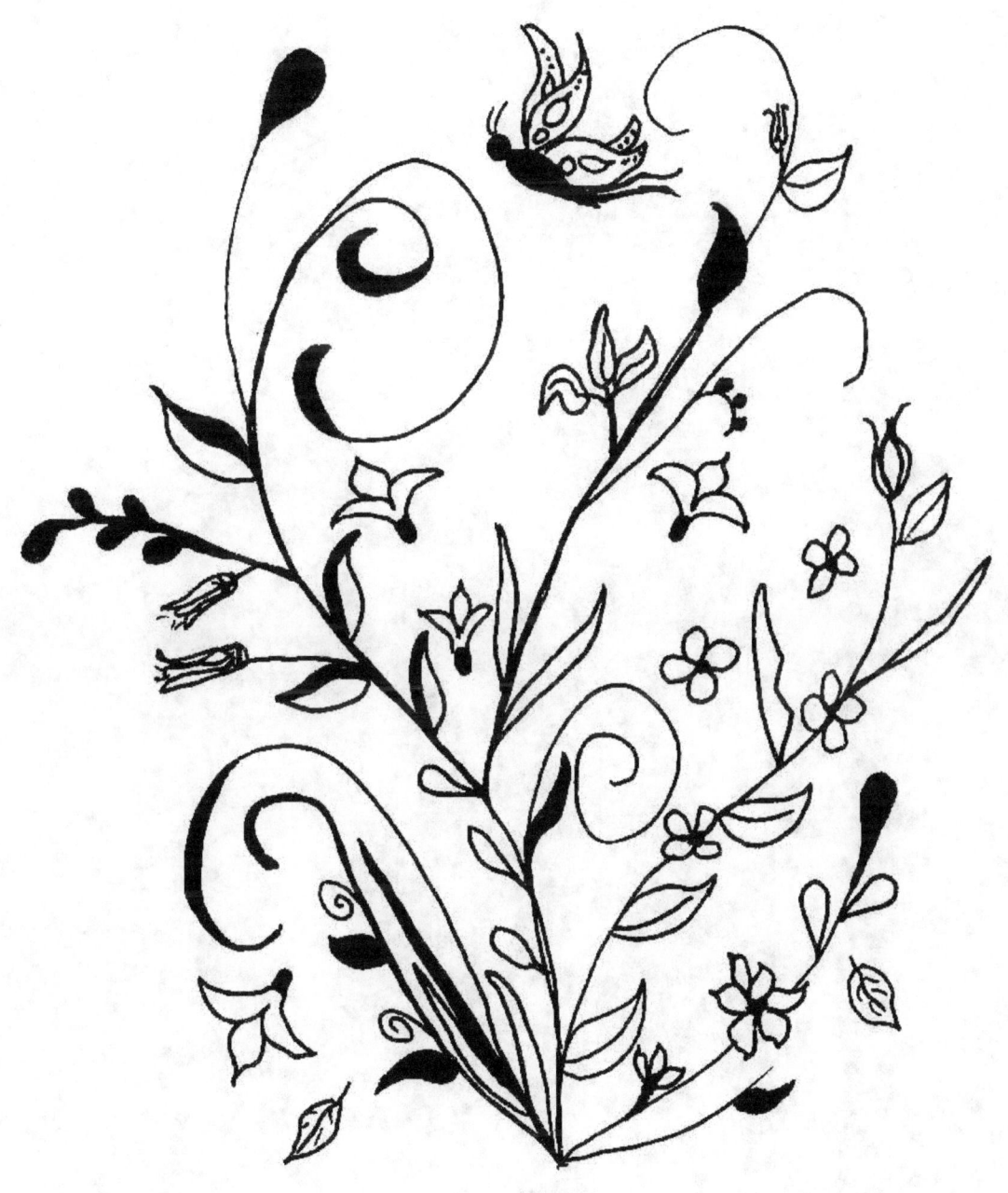

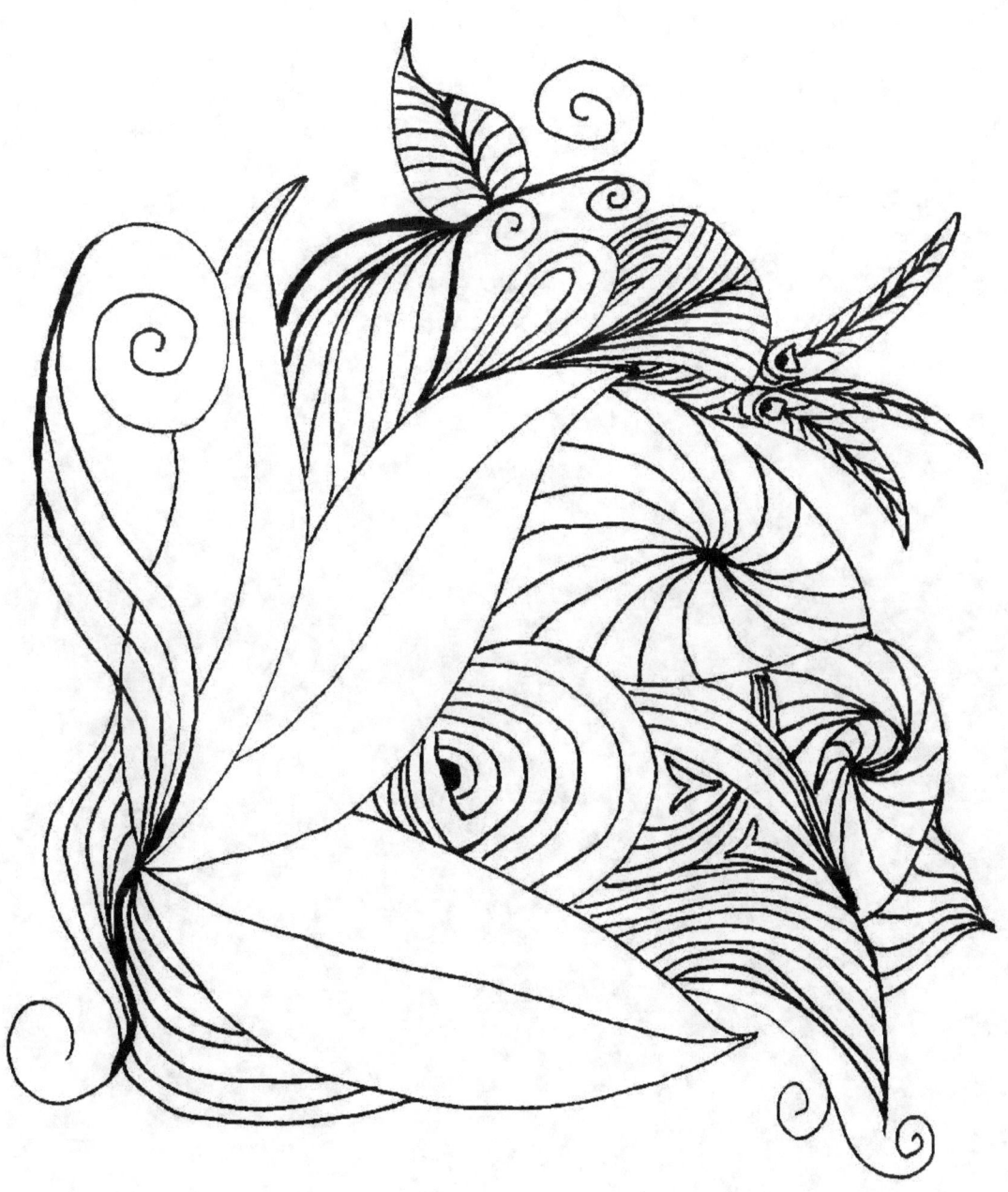

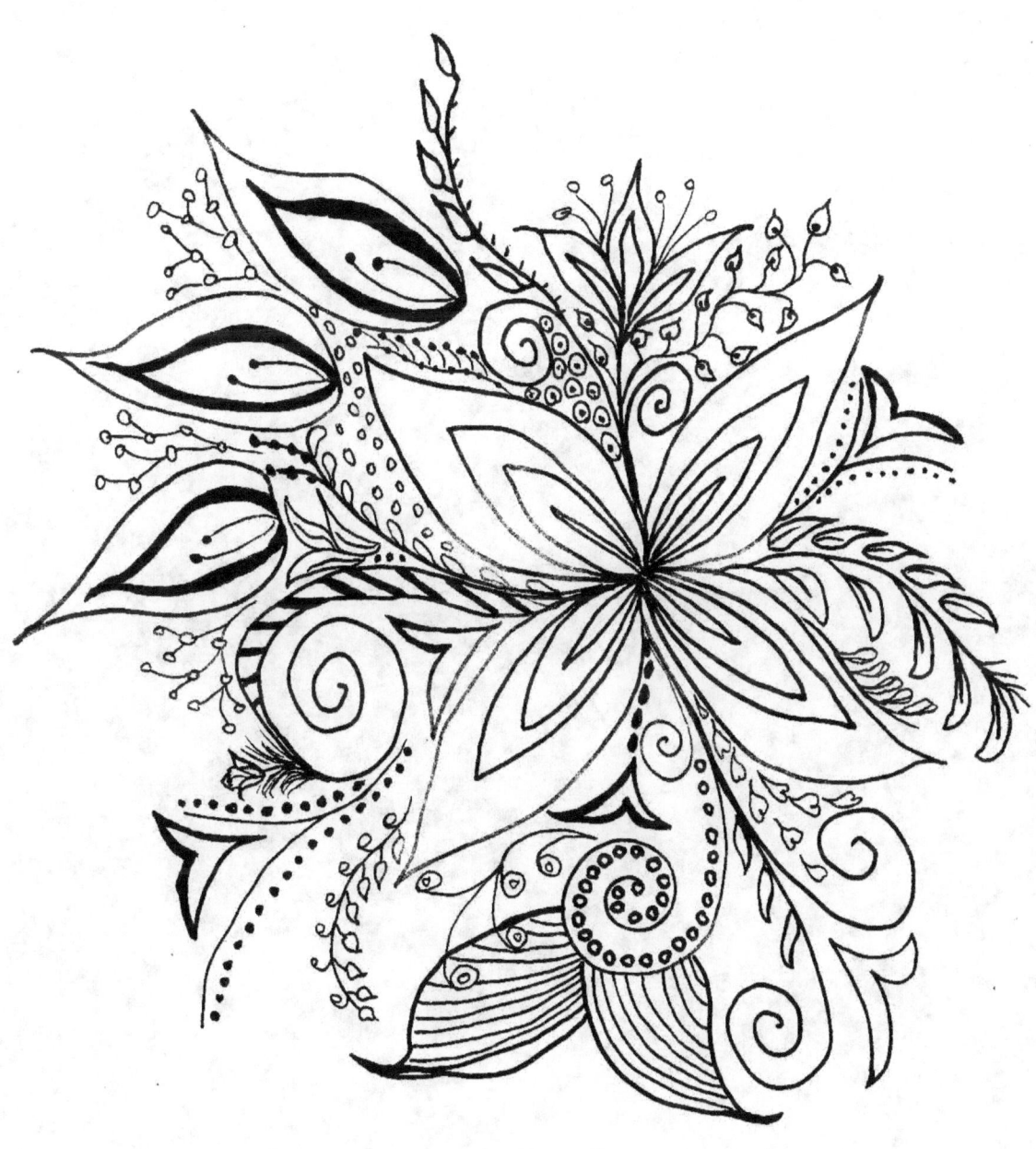

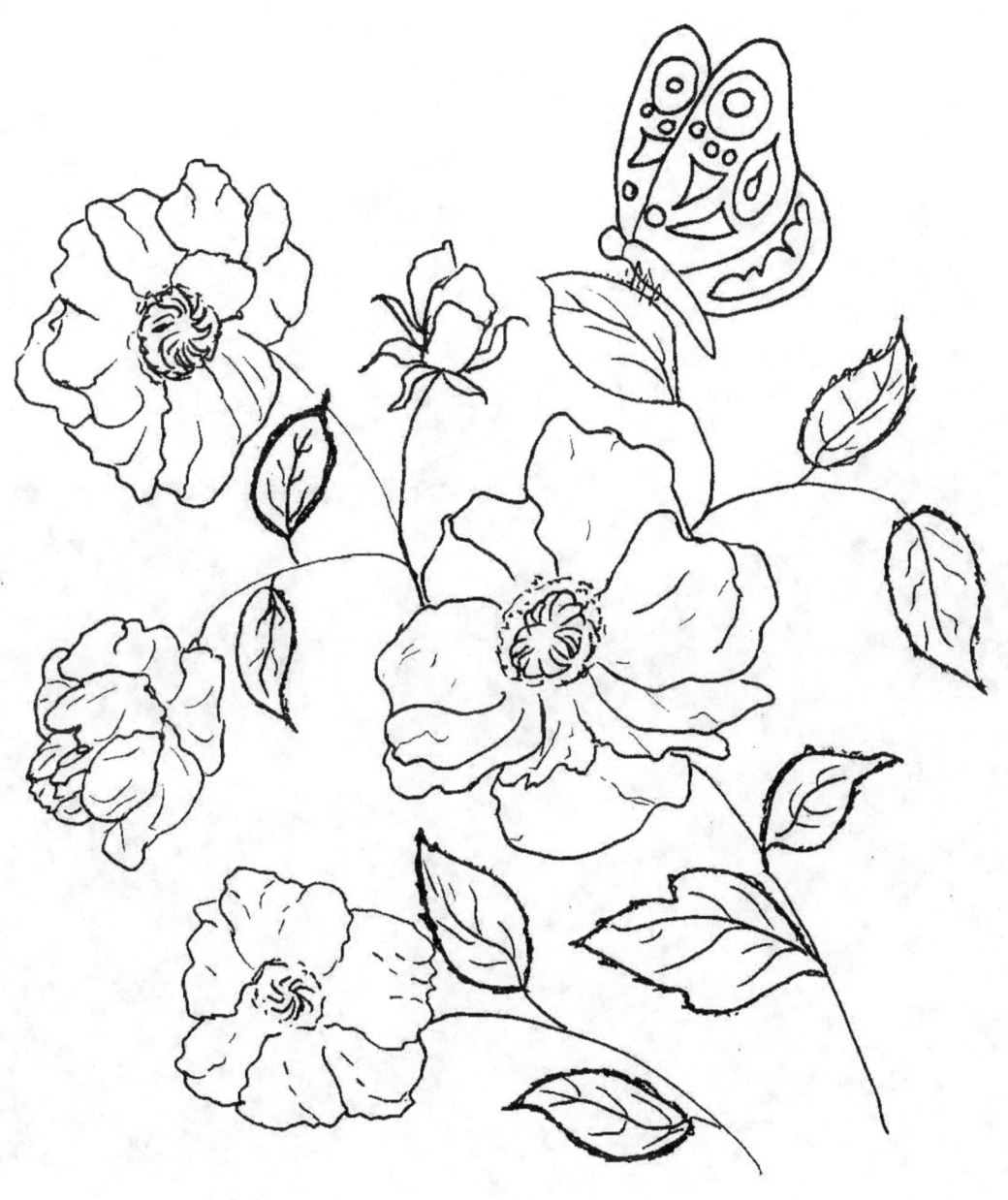

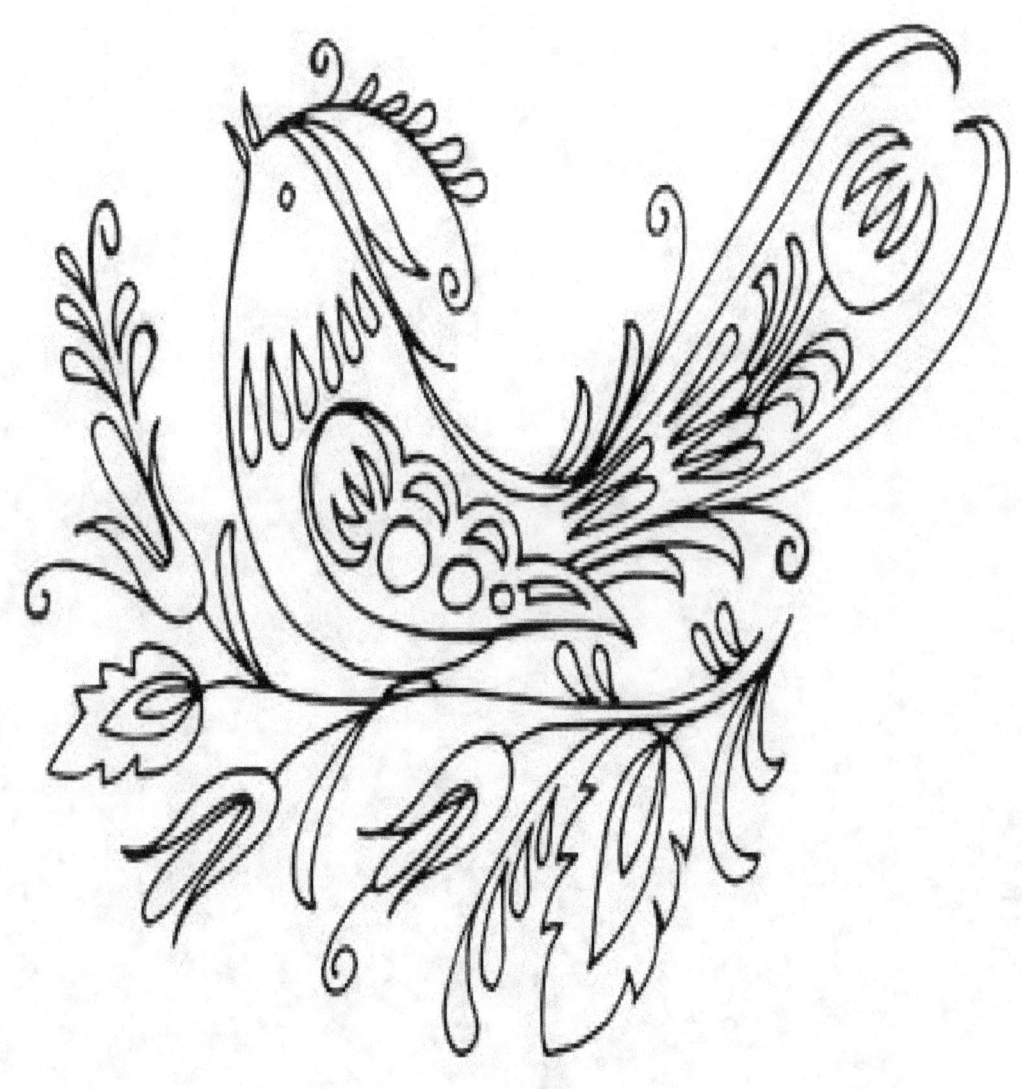

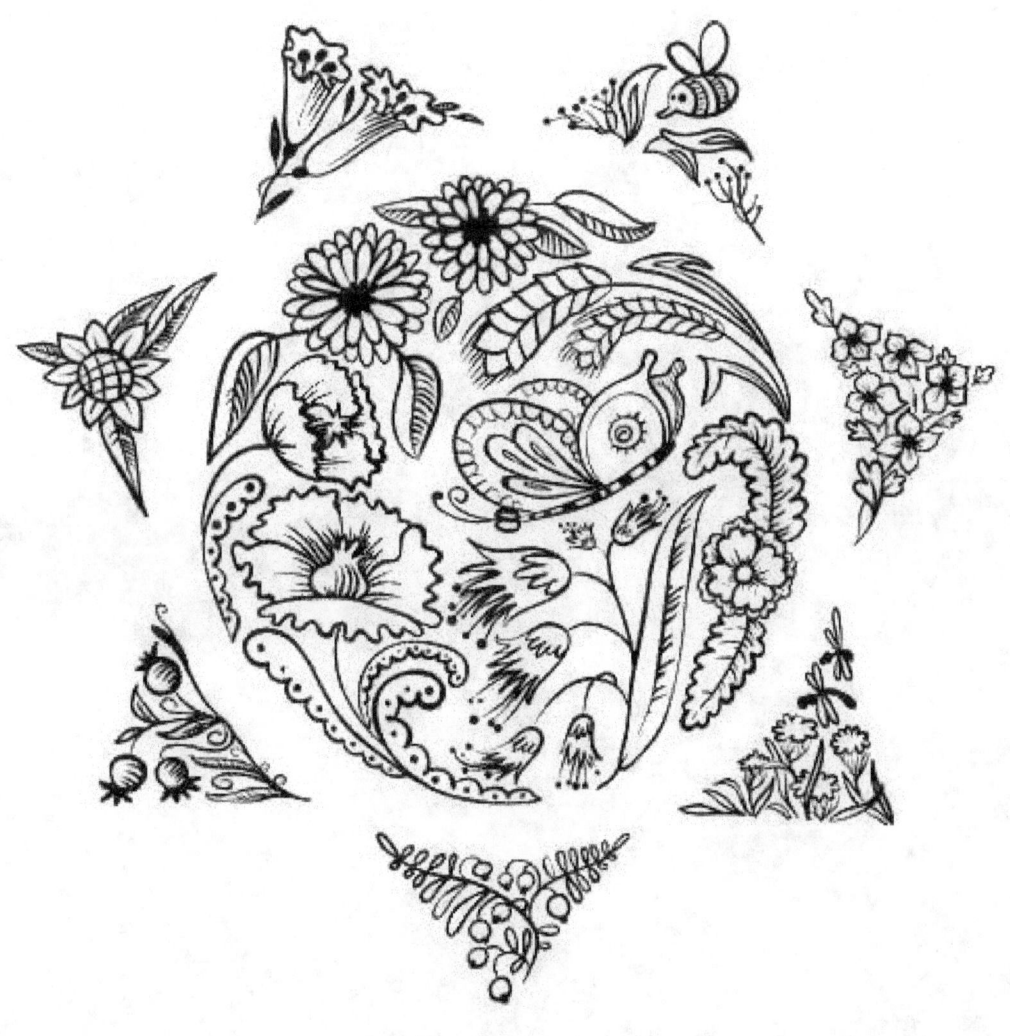

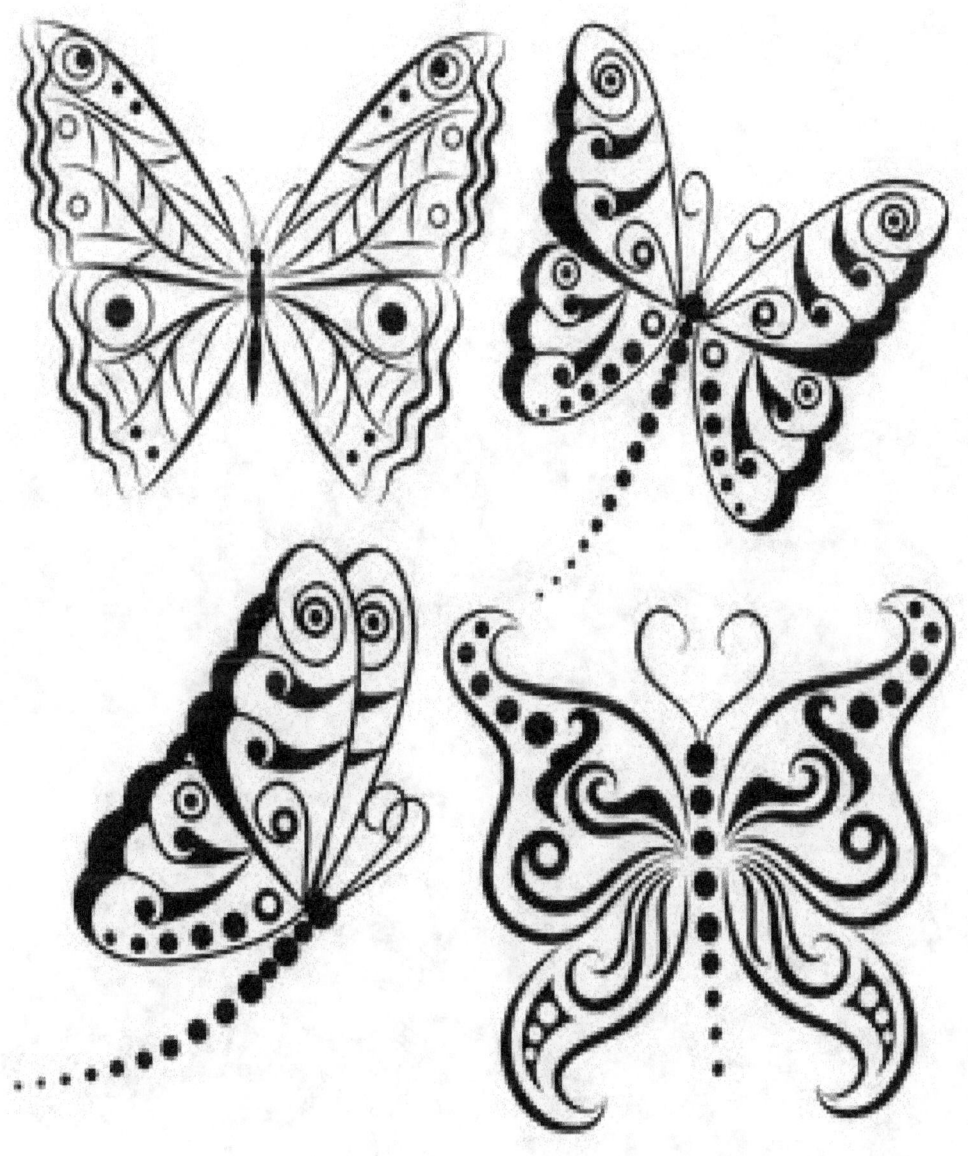

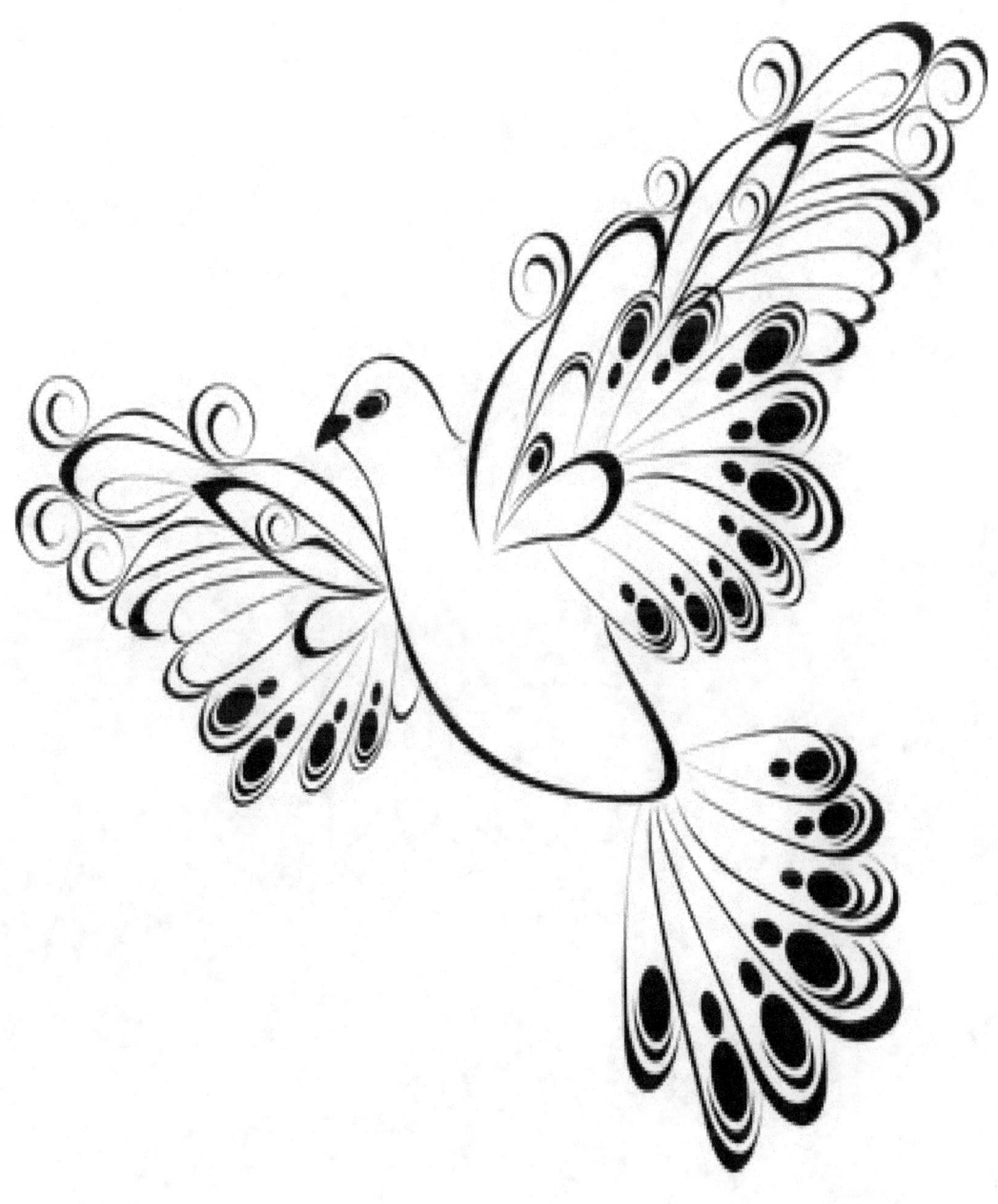

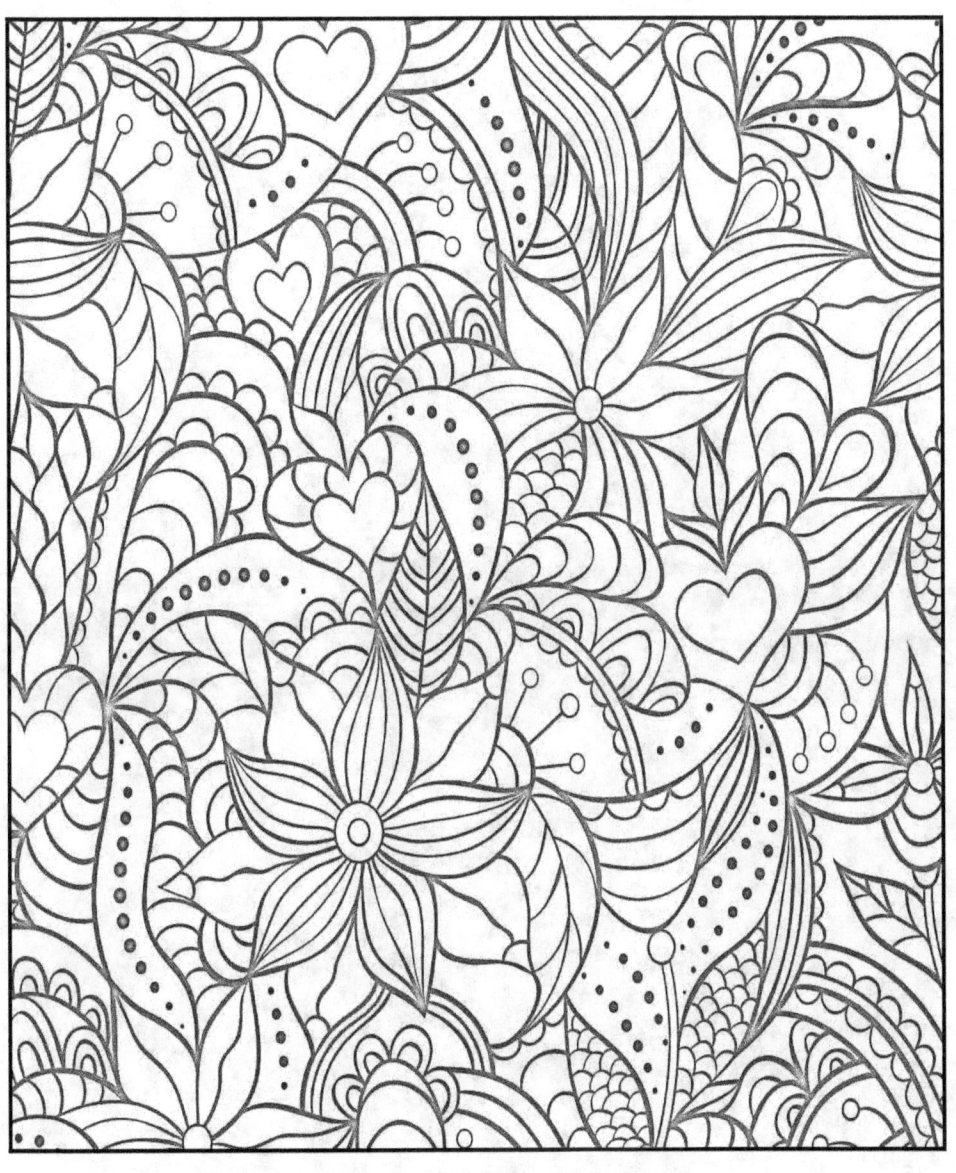

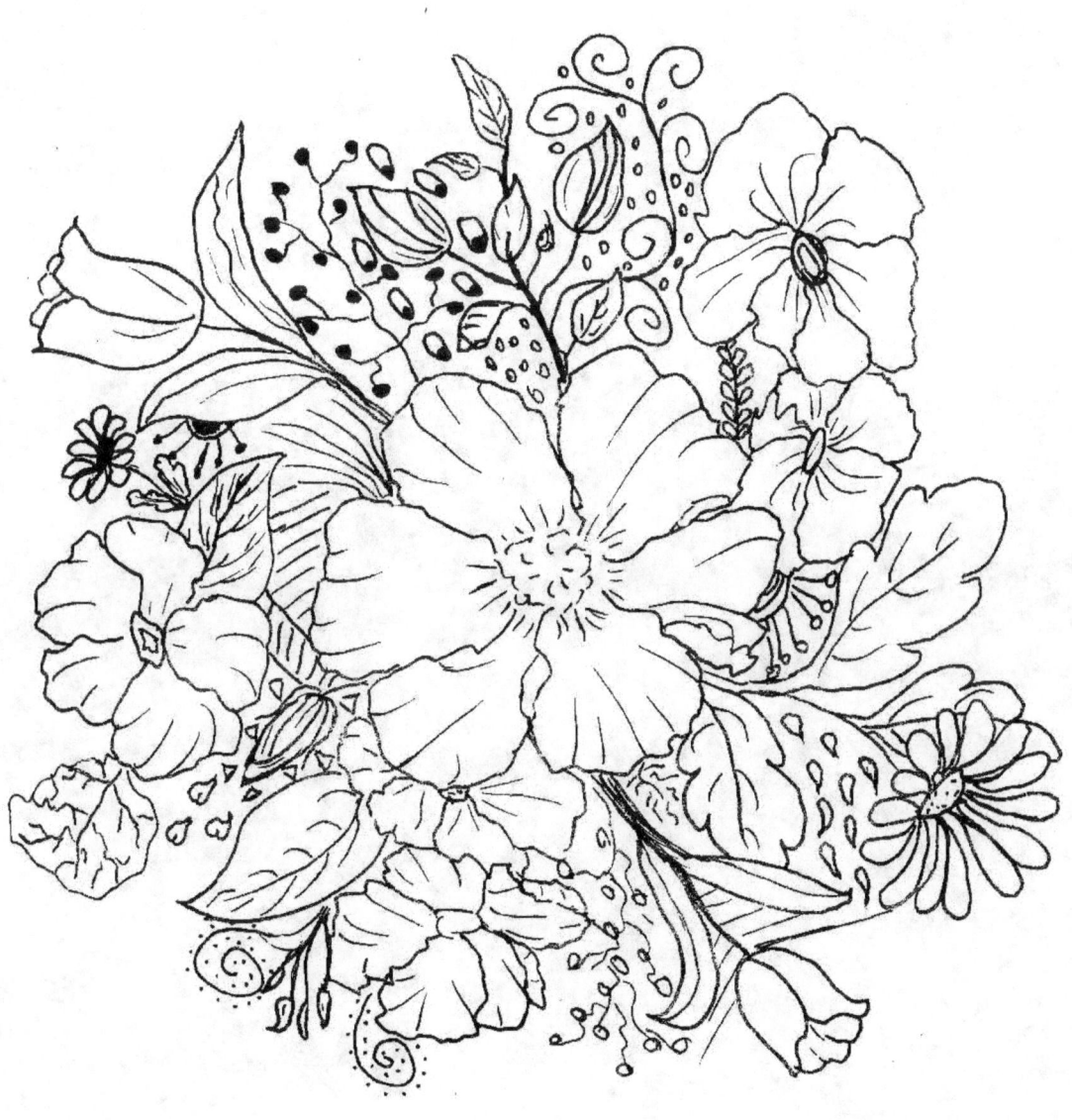

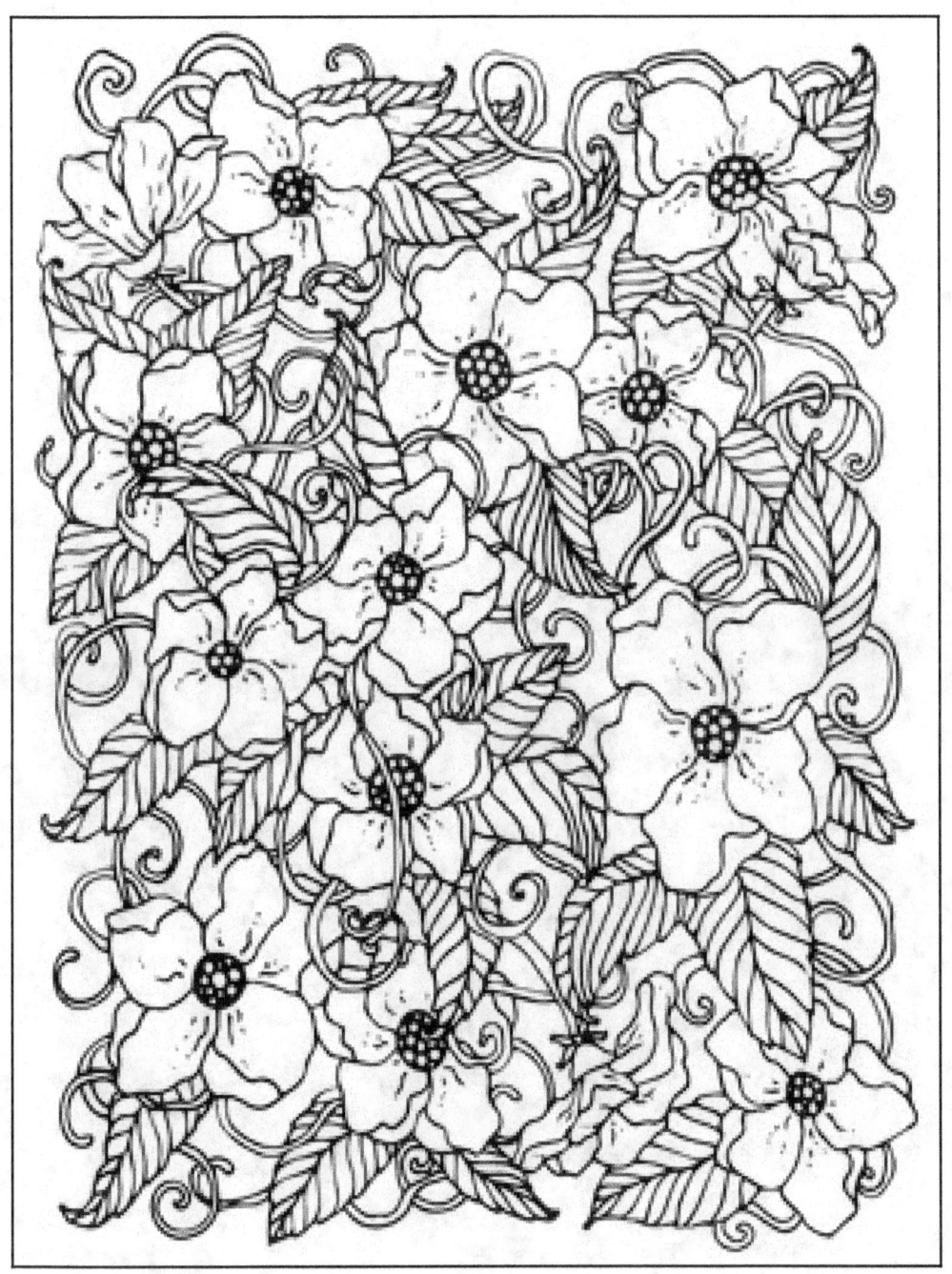

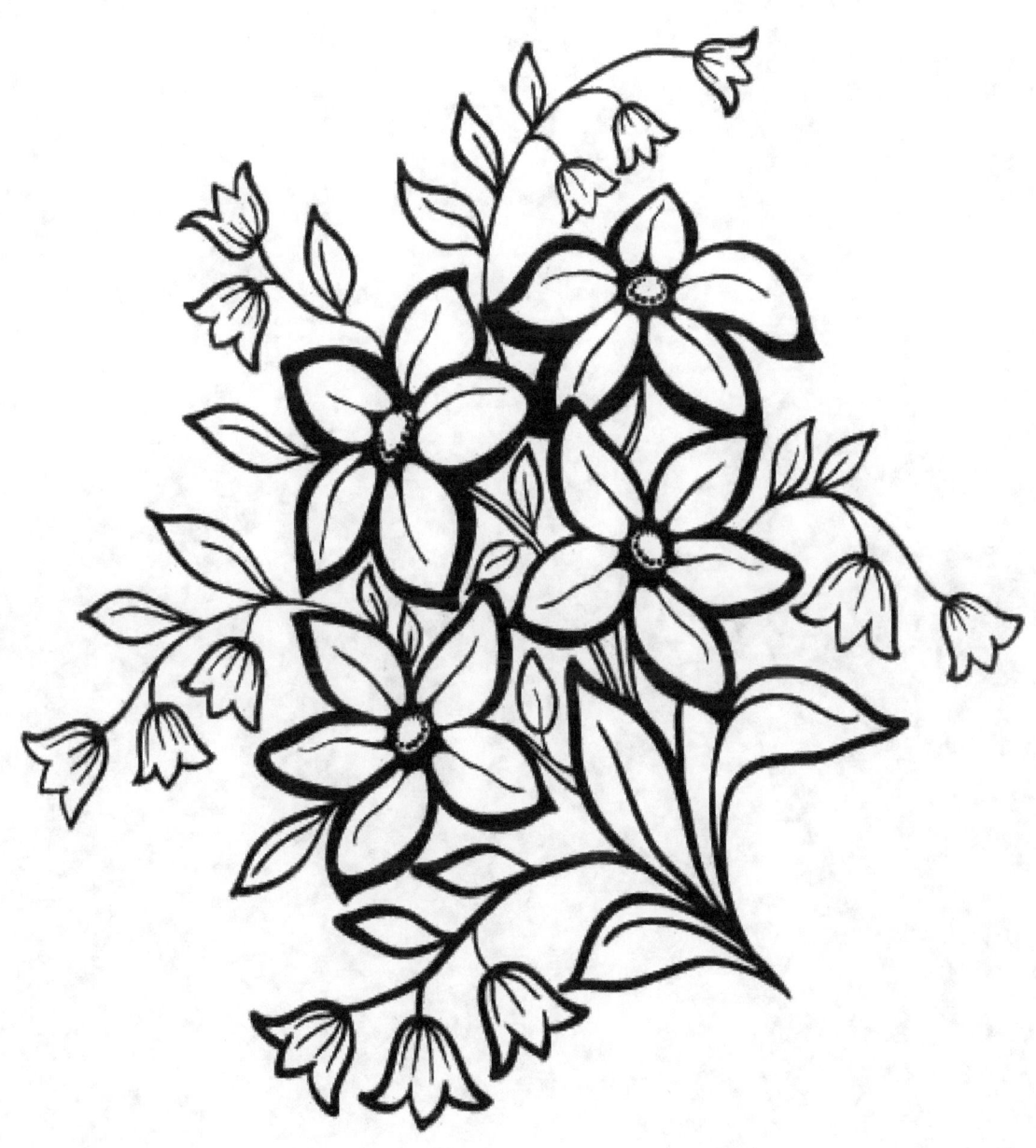

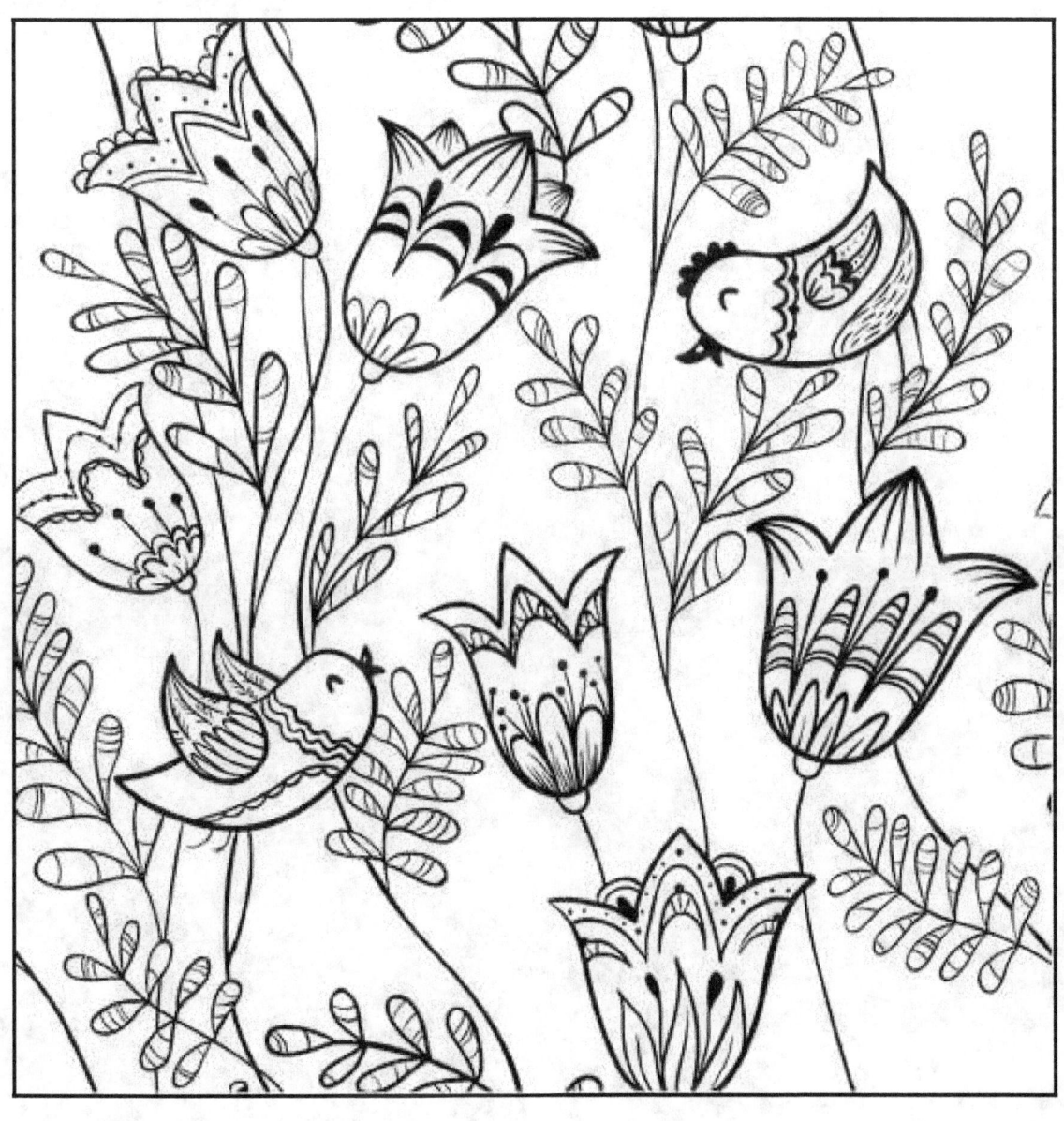

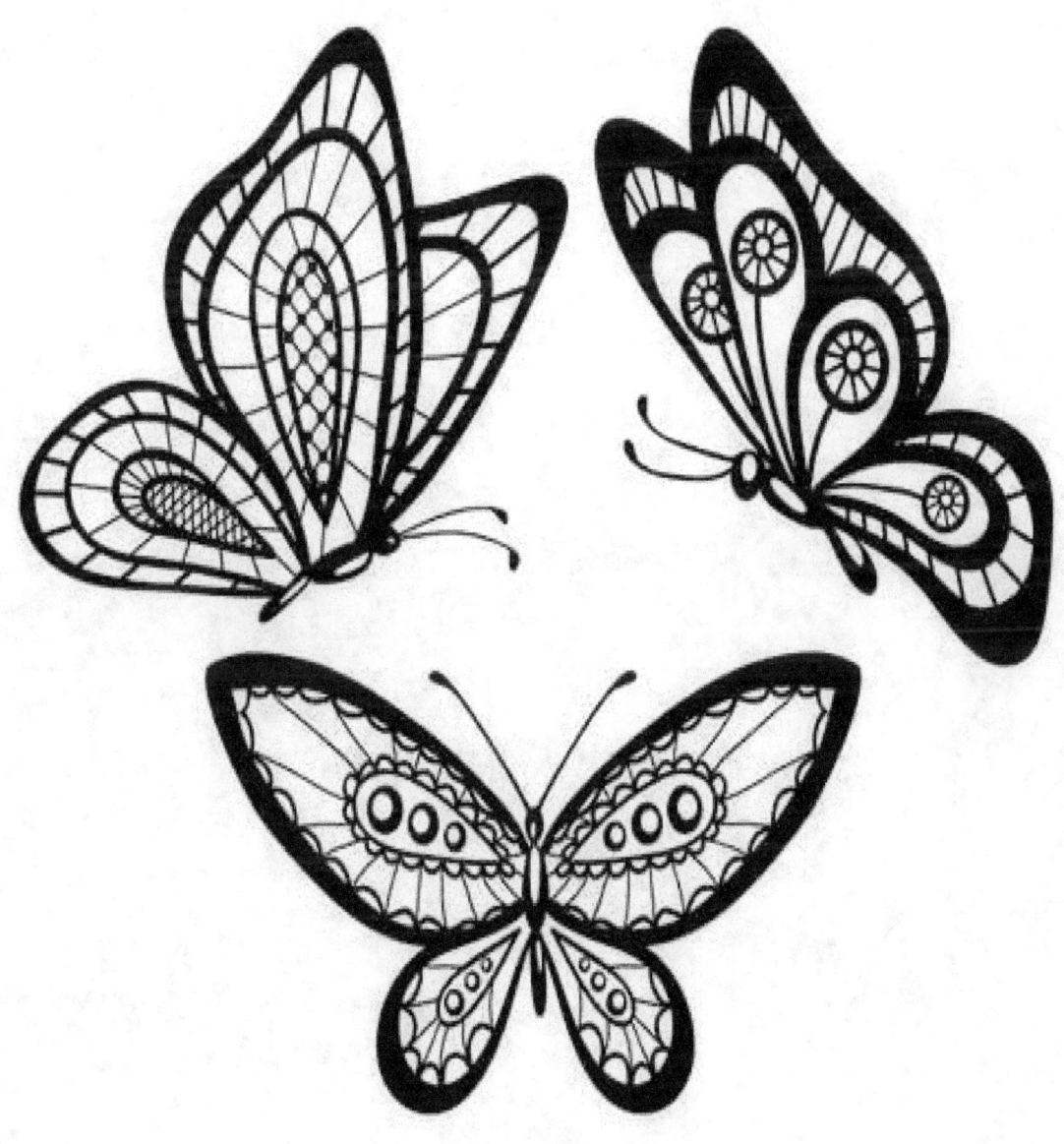

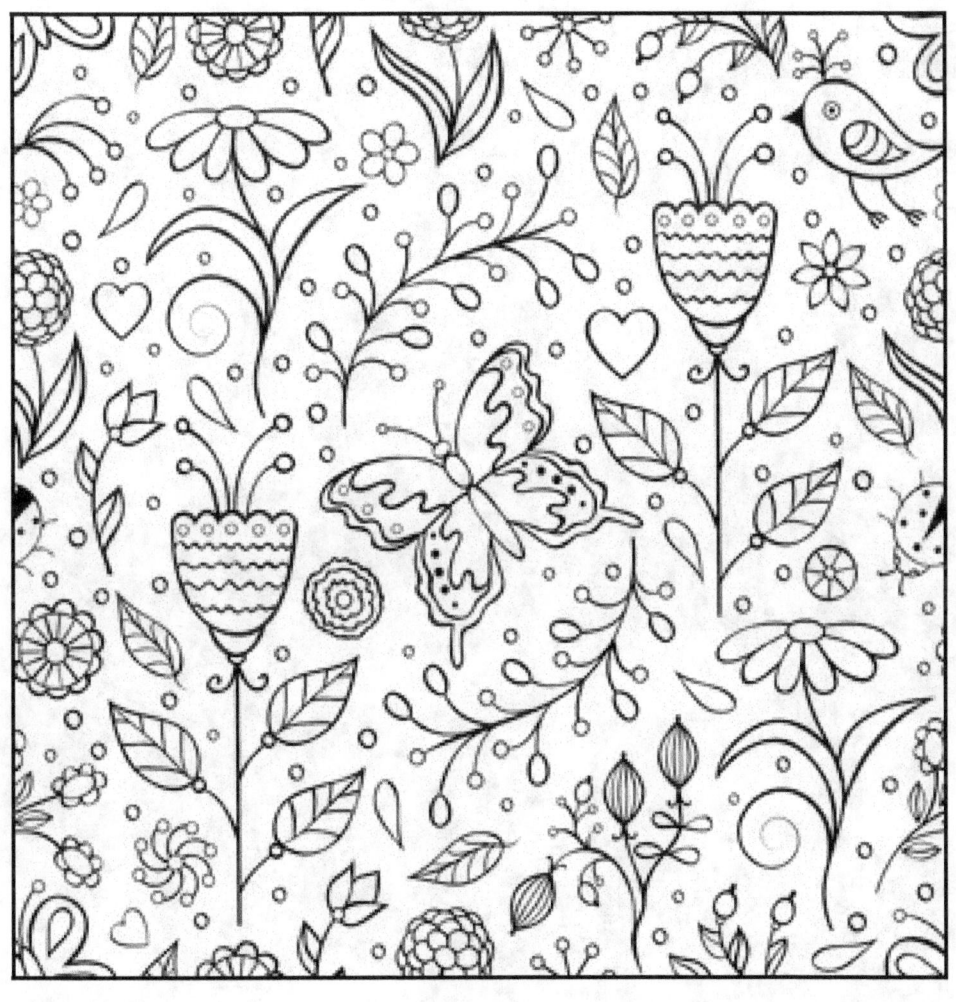

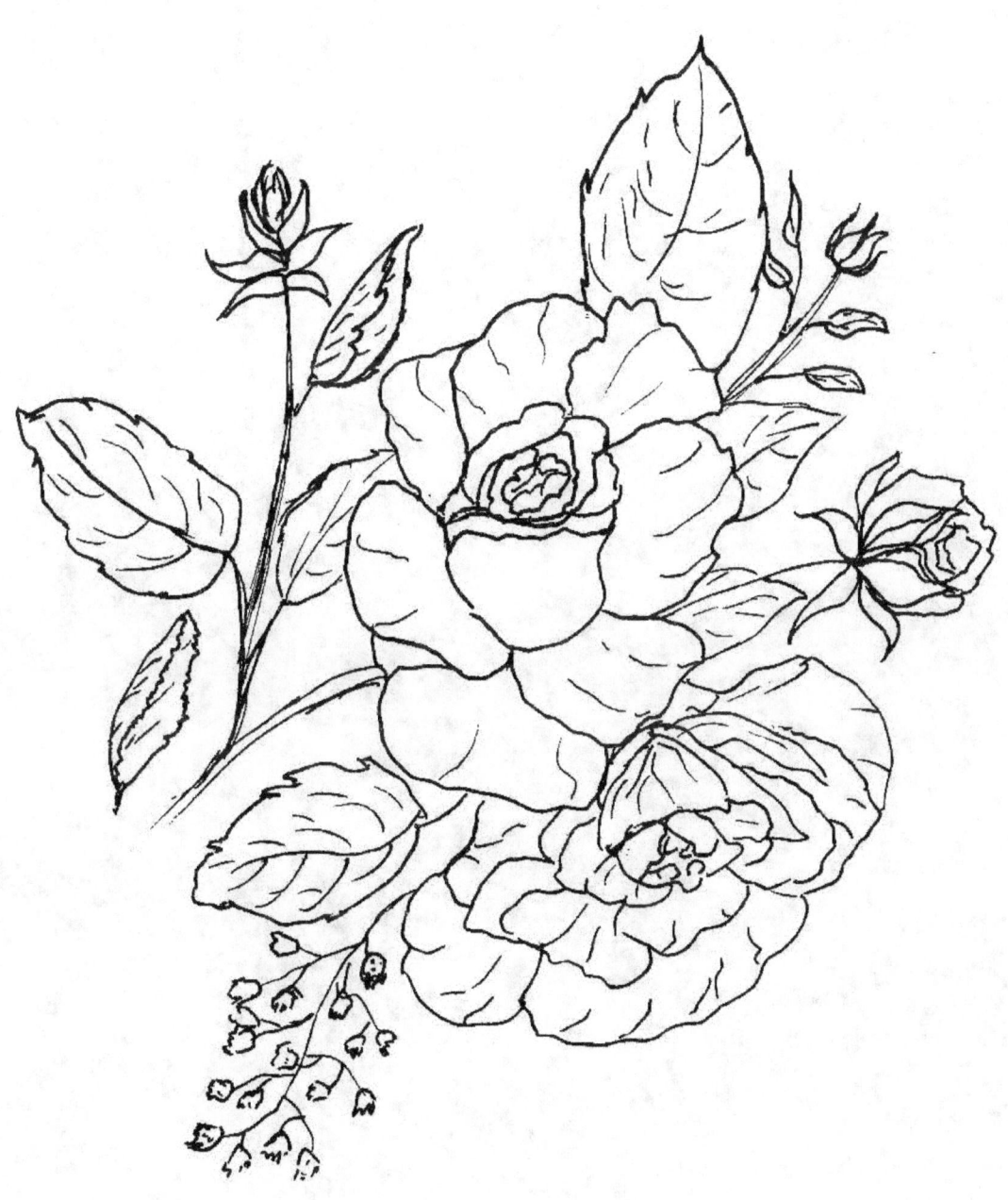

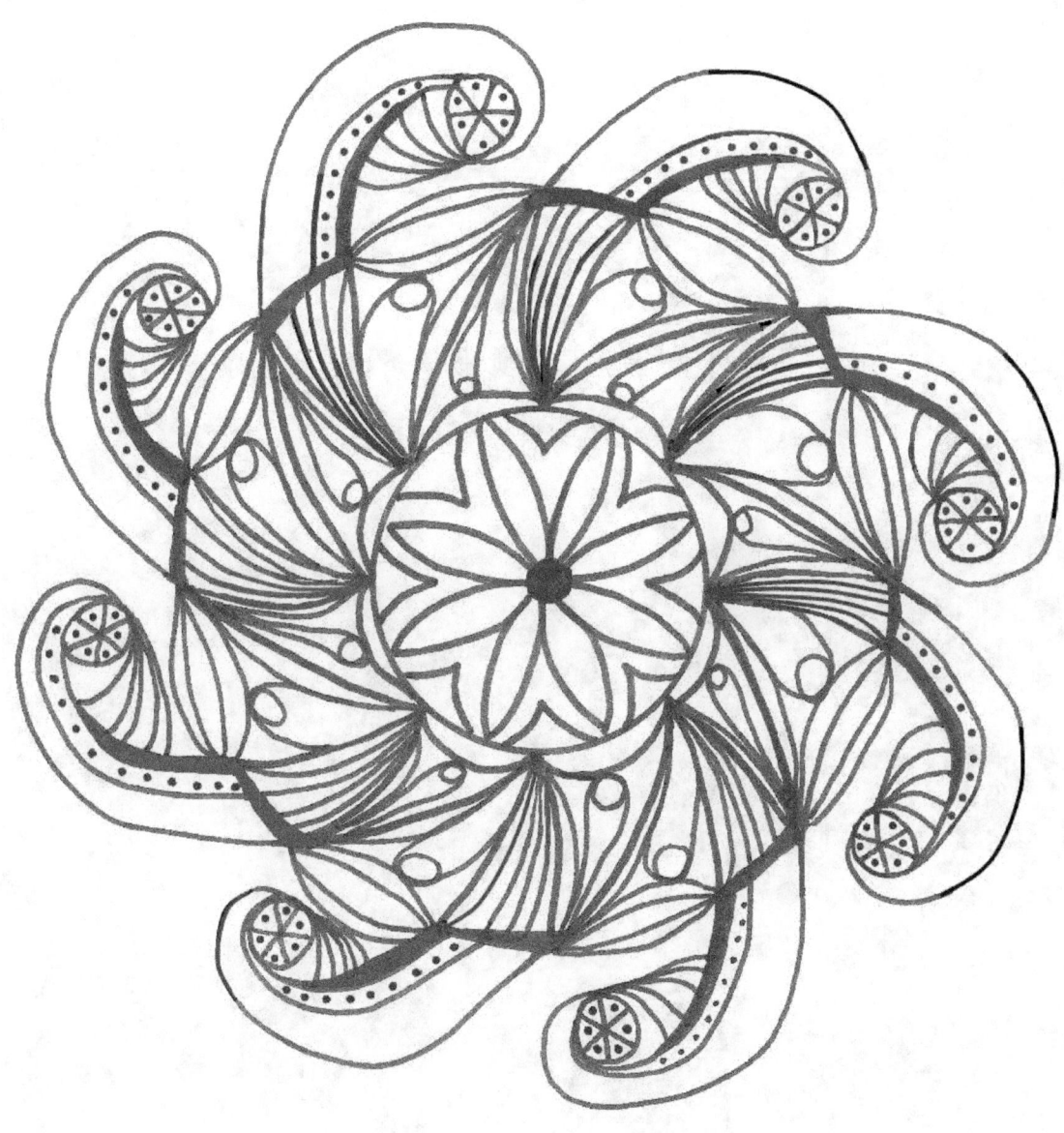

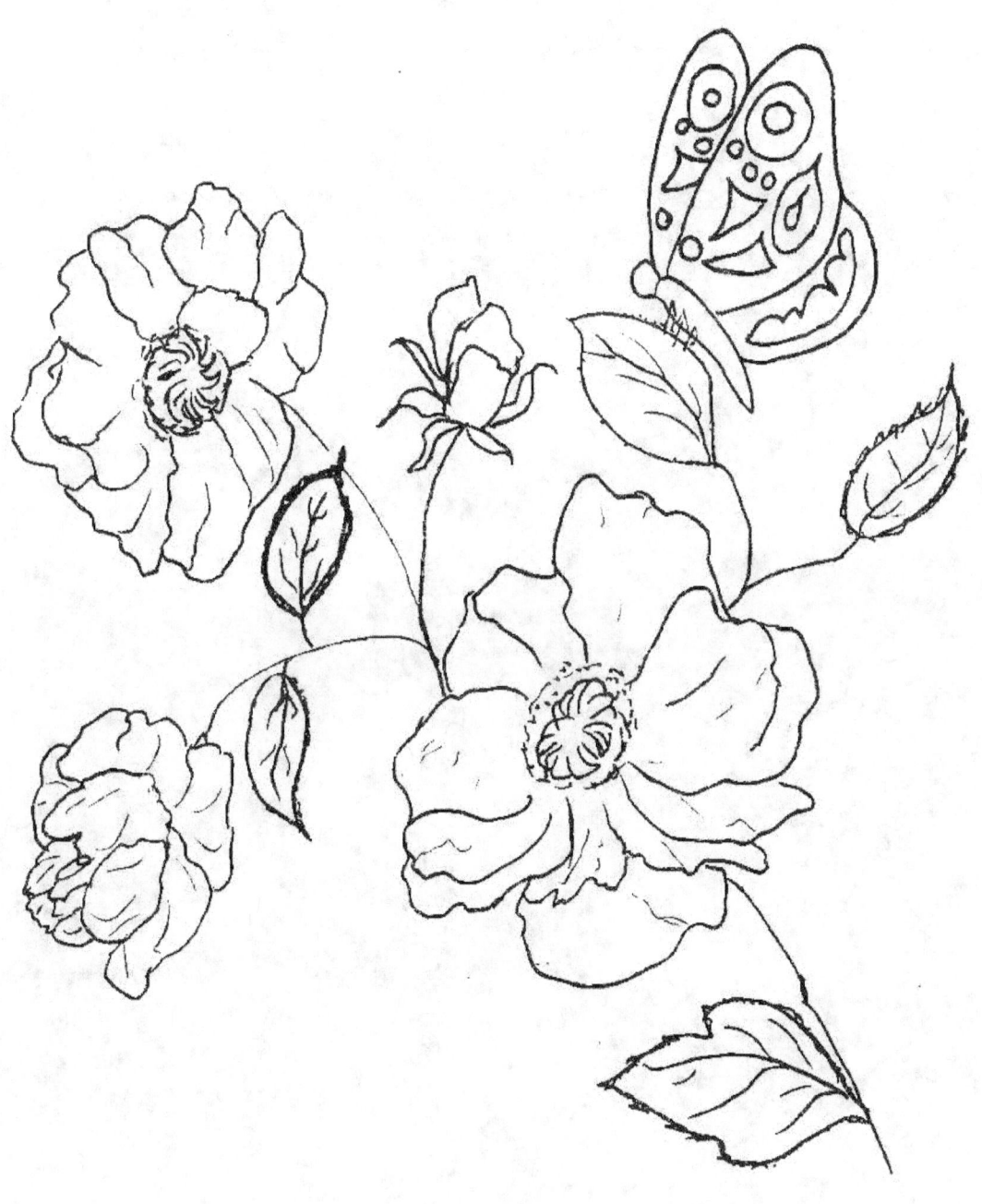

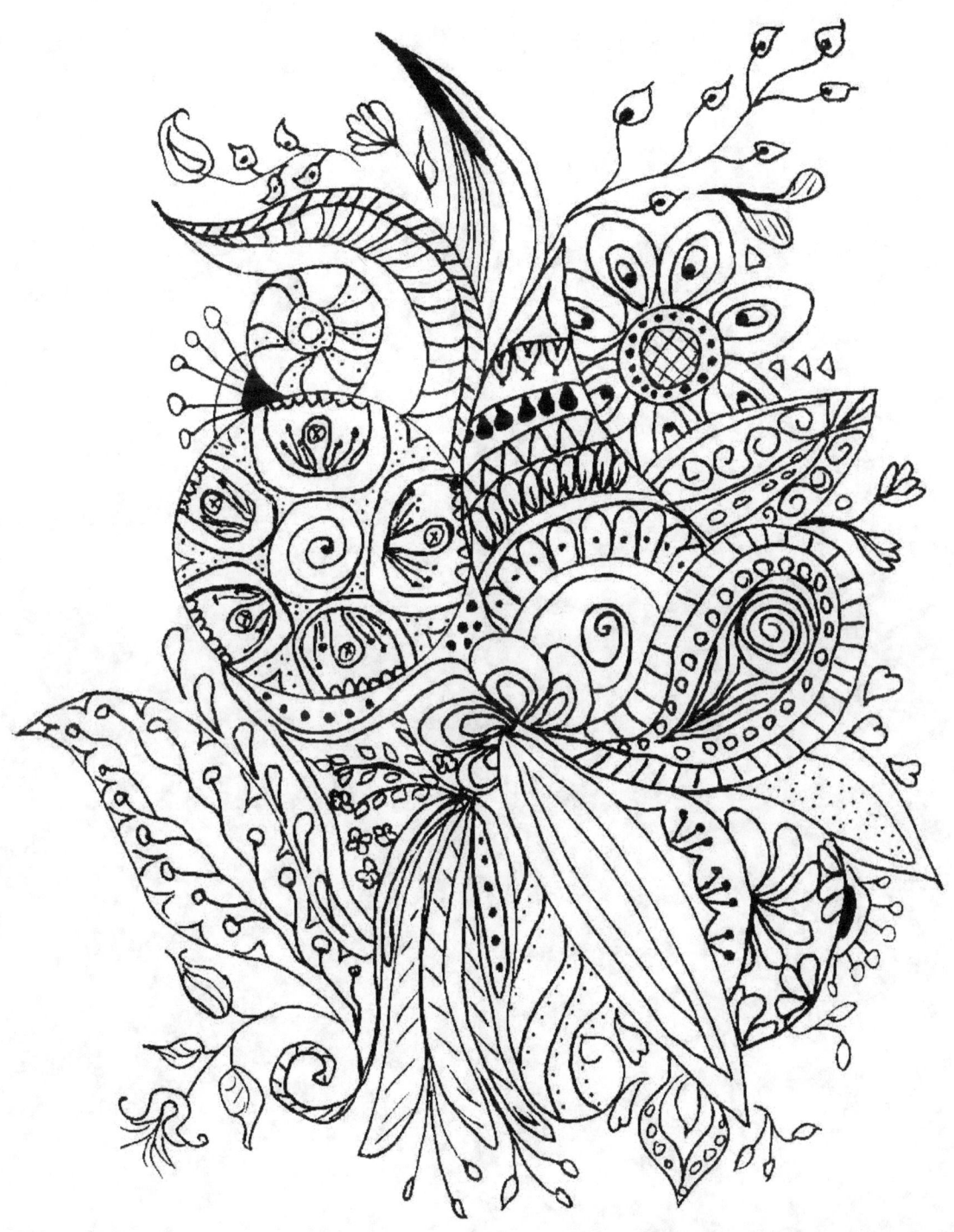

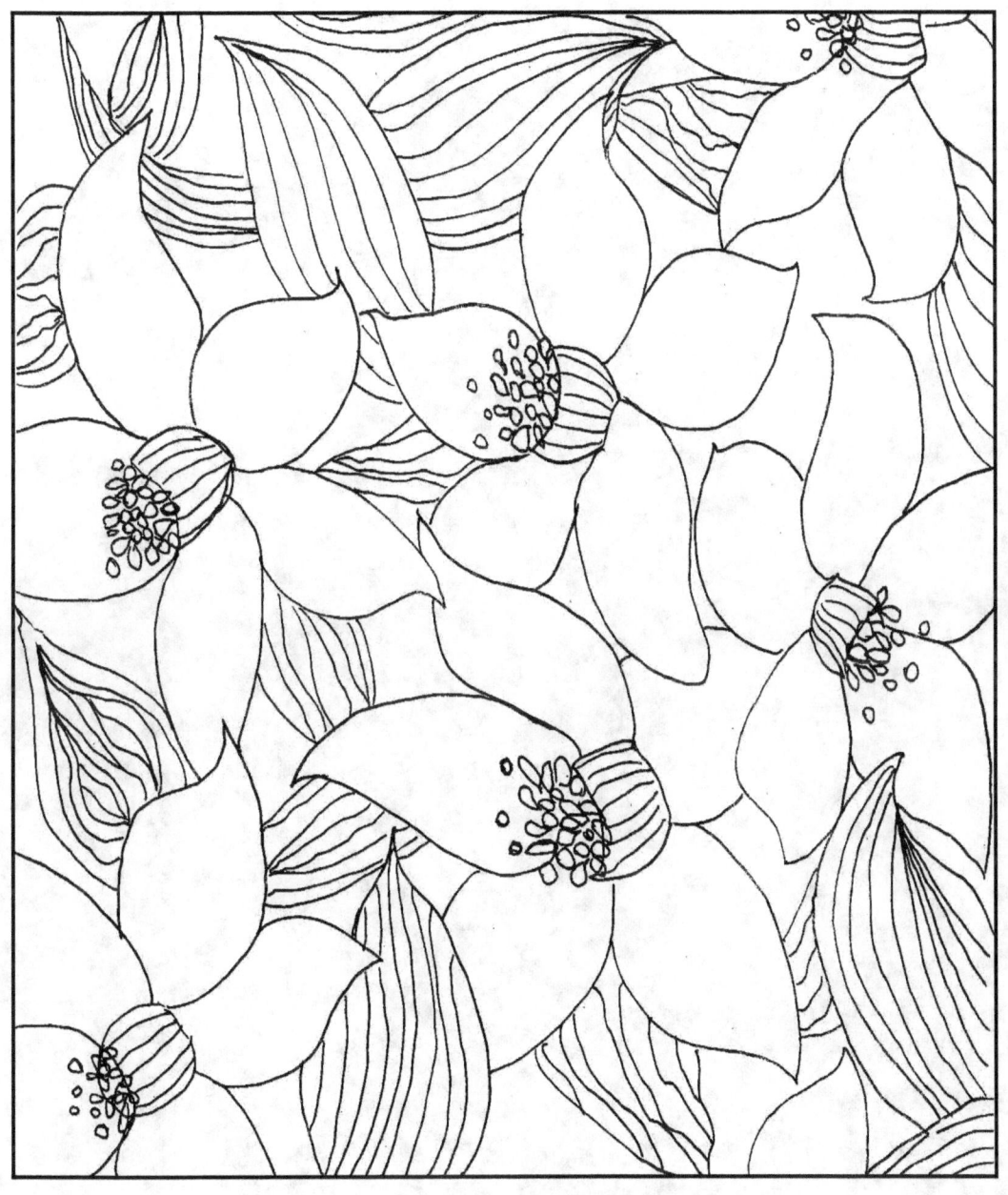

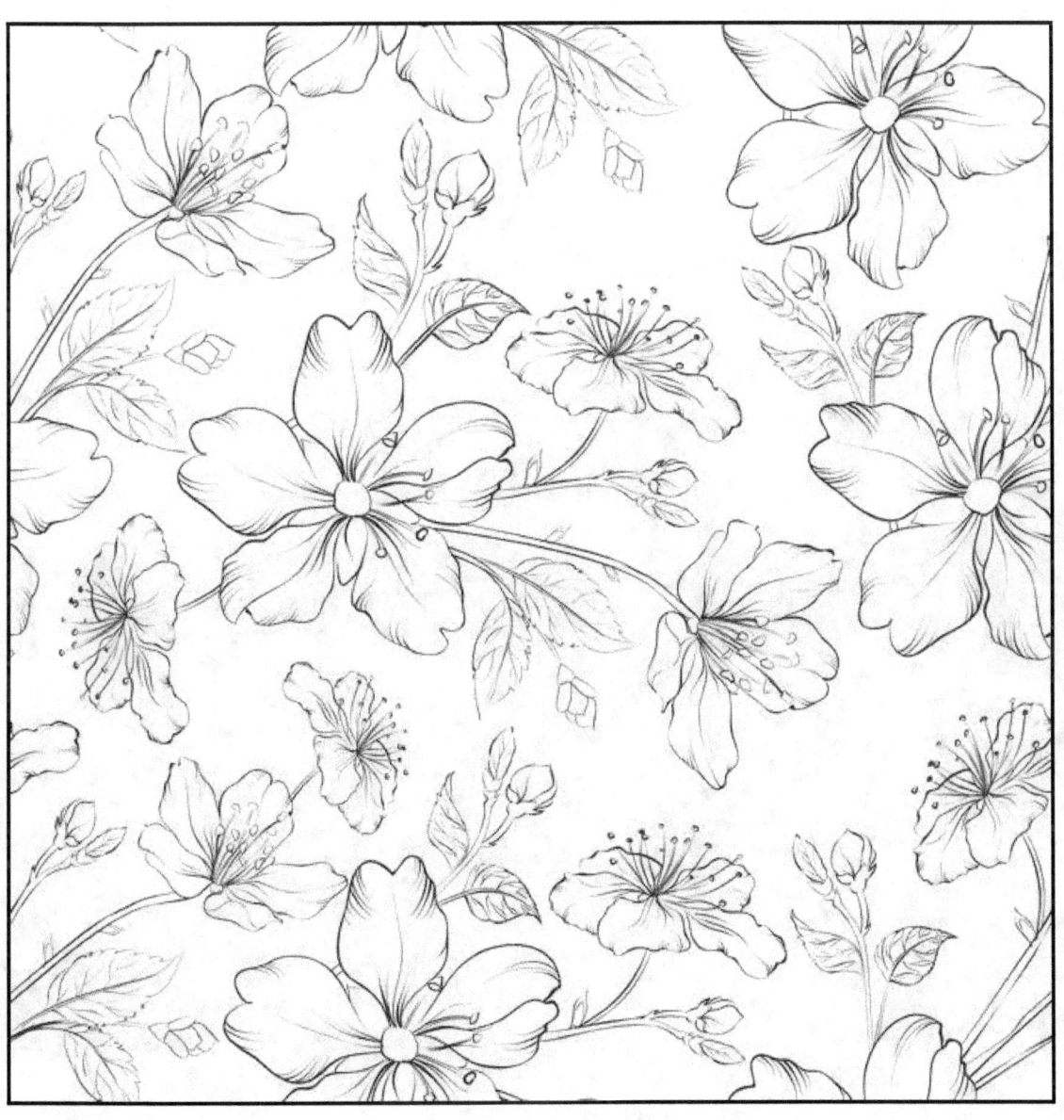

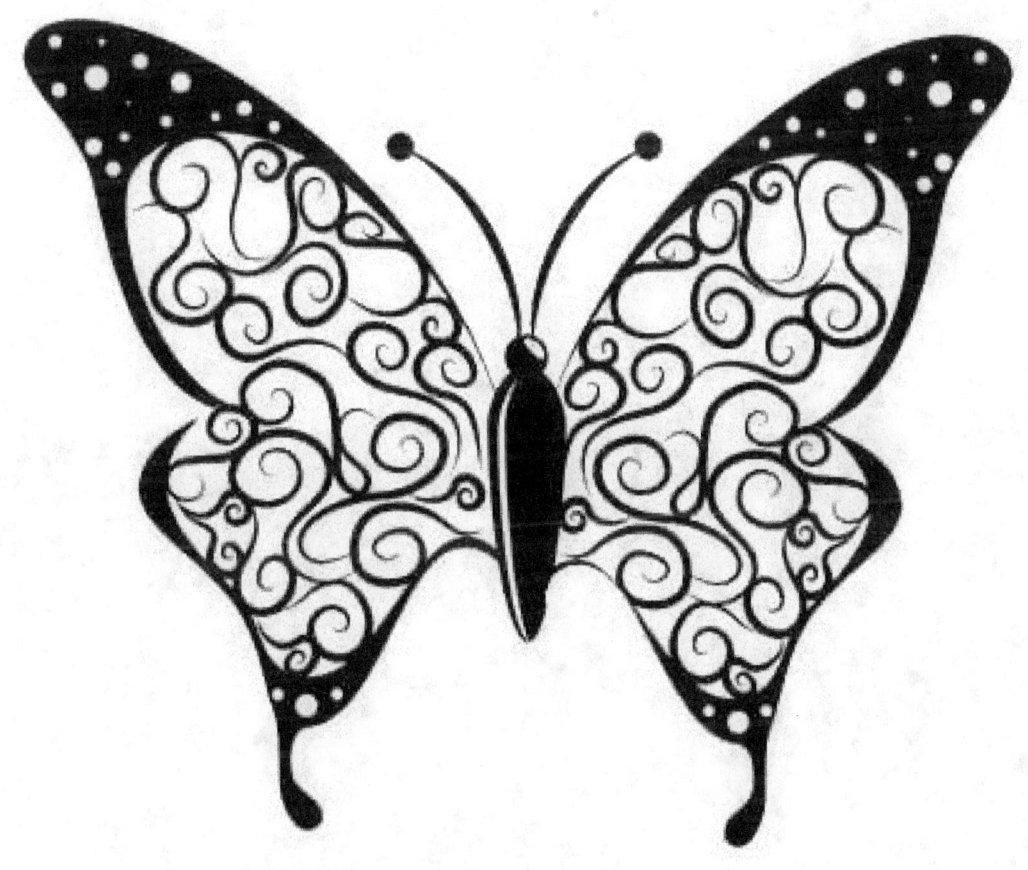

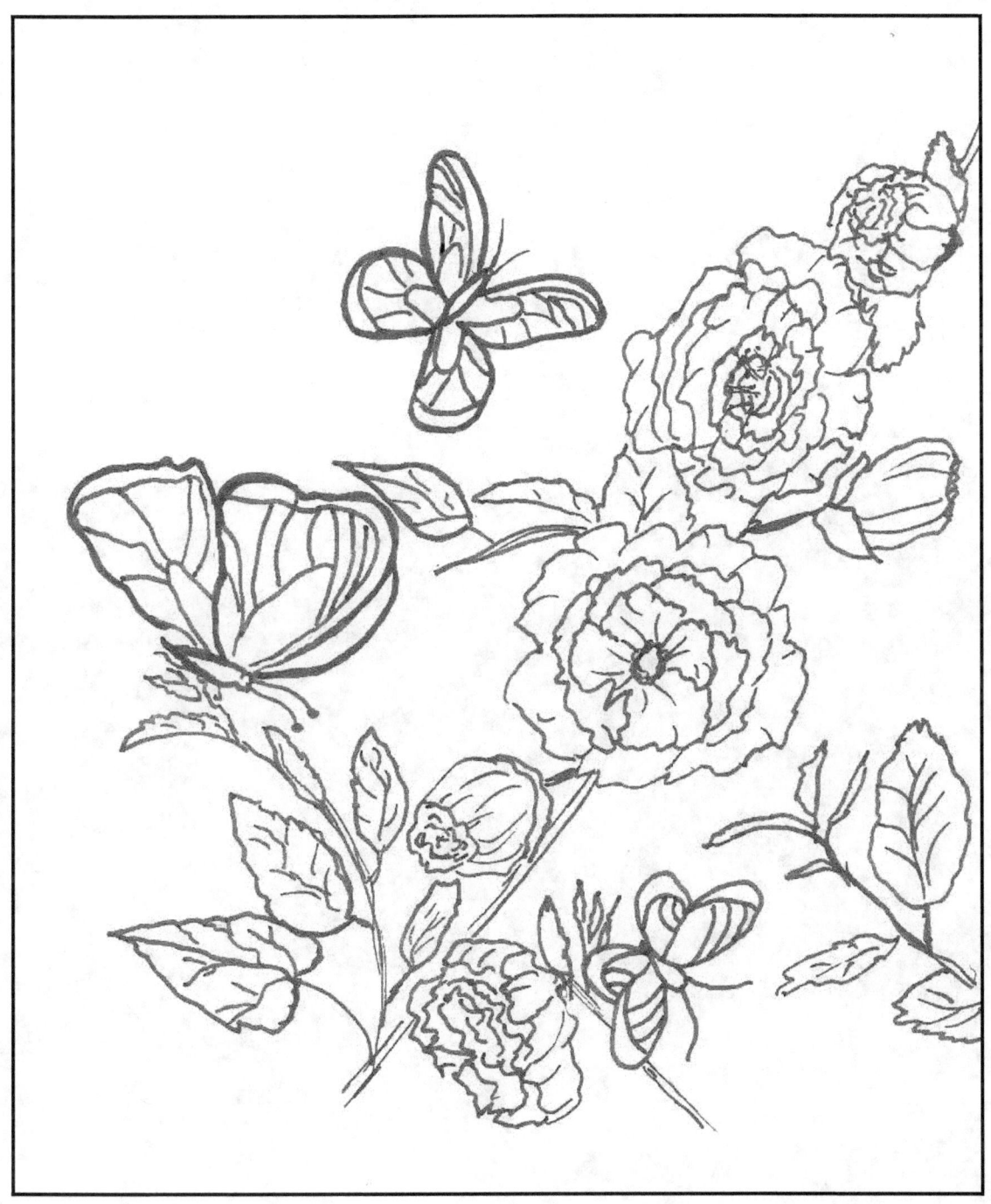

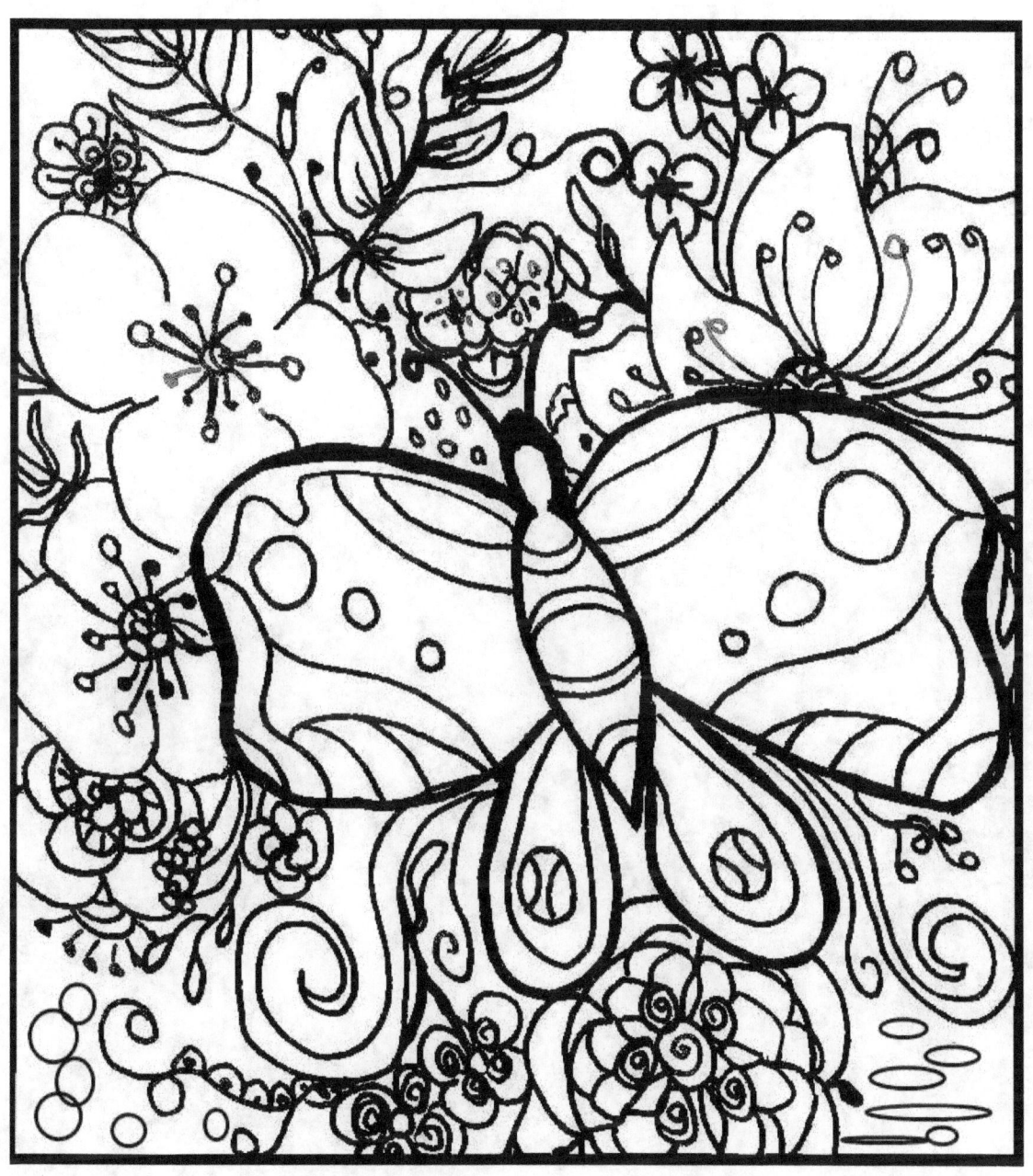

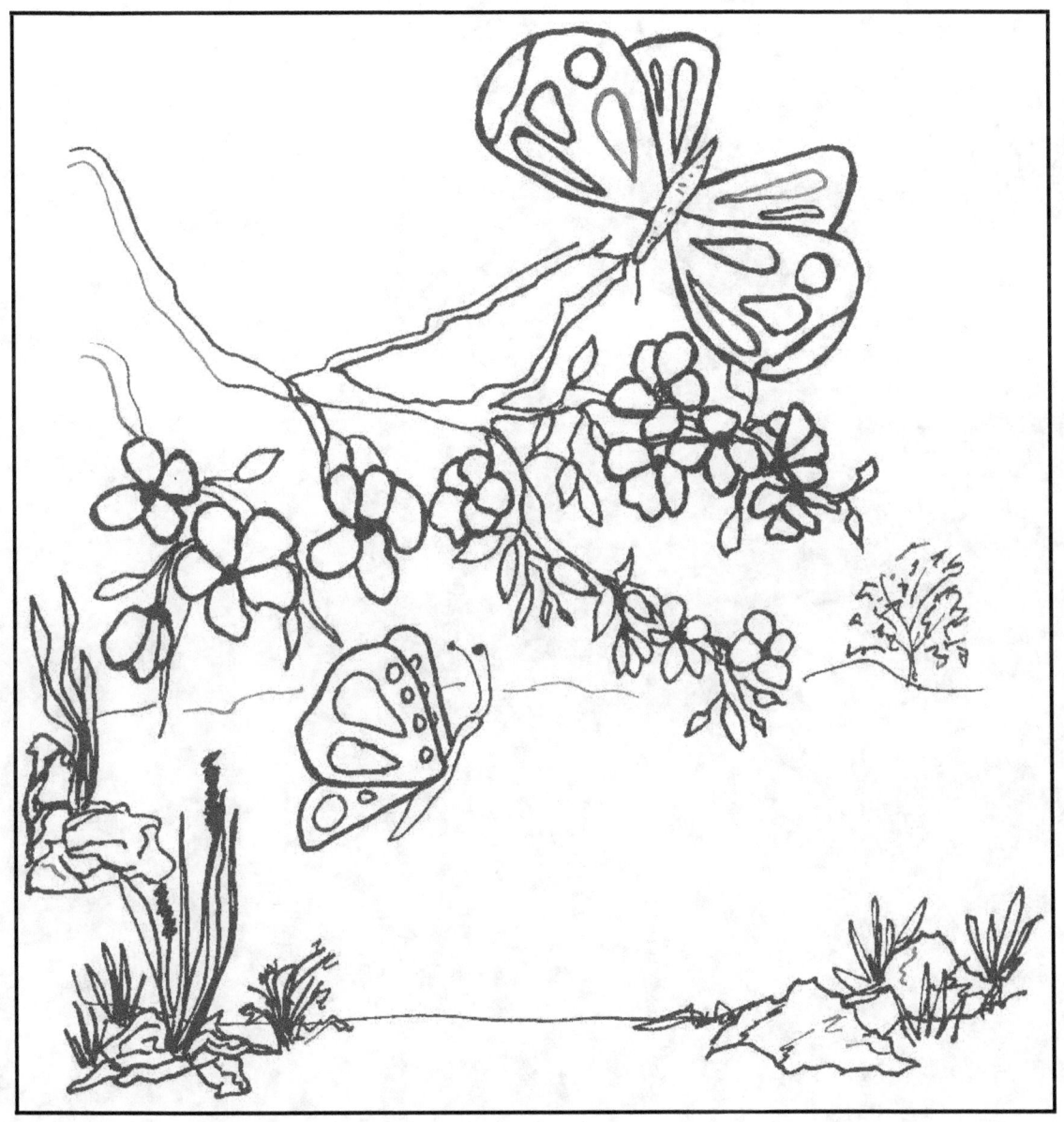

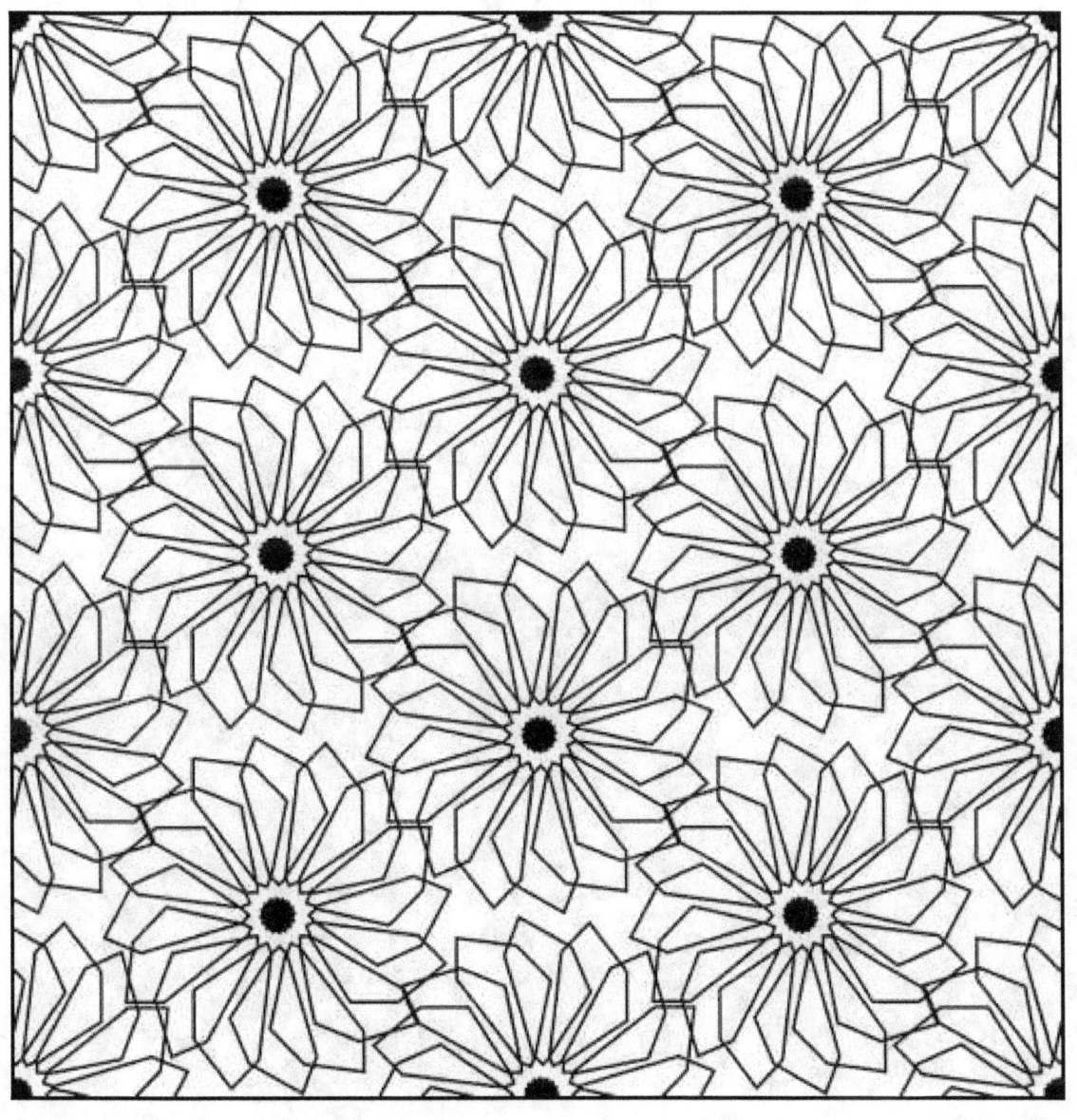

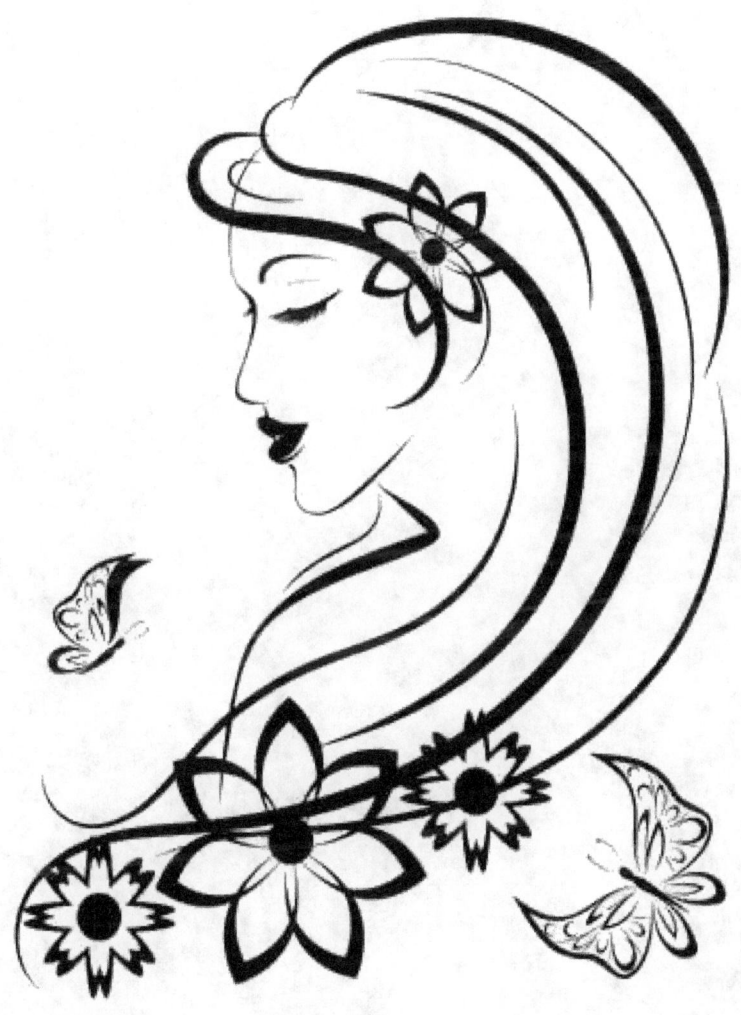

Adult Coloring Books -

Julia Brockmann

https://www.createspace.com

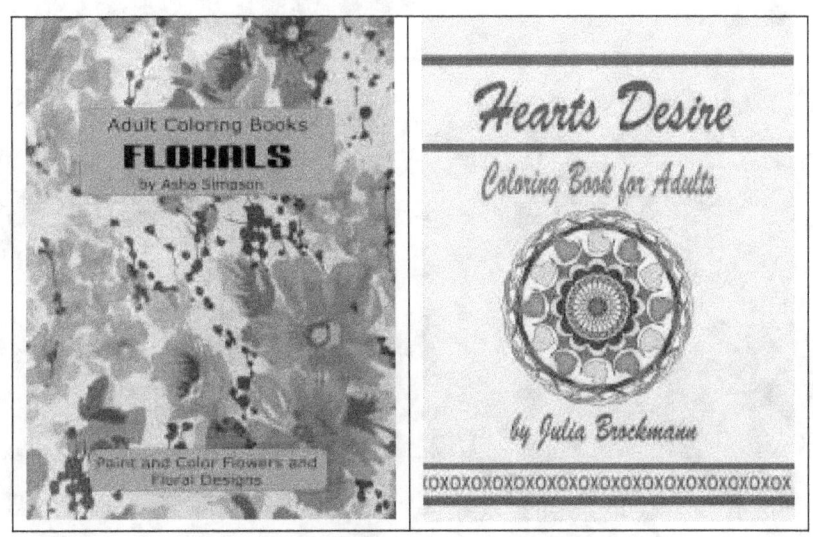

Published through

KD Coloring Studio

http://kdcoloring.com

KD Coloring also lists adult coloring books by other artists.